Memoirs of a Swedish War Nurse

A Life of Adventure, A Journey to Spirituality

Karin Wiking

An Interview
by Lois Lindstrom

Published in conjunction witih
Goose River Press
Waldoboro, Maine

Library of Congress Control Number: 2002105404

ISBN: 1-930648-34-0

Second Printing, 2002.

Published in conjunction with
Goose River Press
3400 Friendship Road
Waldoboro, Maine 04572
e mail: dbenner@ime.net

Memoirs of a Swedish War Nurse:
A Life of Adventure, A Journey to Spirituality

Karin Wiking interviewed by Lois Lindstrom

Prologue

Sometimes a good story is hard to get. Sometimes it just falls by the wayside. Sometimes it starts as one thing and becomes another.

That's what happened when I interviewed Sweden's Karin Wiking. Every couple of weeks, we got together for tea at Karin's apartment near Stockholm and talked about her past. In the beginning, I was most interested in her work as a war nurse for the Swedish Red Cross in the 1940s. In the end, I was seeking Karin's answers to life's major problems. I had met someone who has faith and is attached to virtuous action.

These interviews usually took place on Saturday—an easy day for both of us to be available. Karin and I, illuminated by natural light peeking through partially closed blinds, would sit together at her dining room table decorated with a small vase of flowers. Religious paintings adorned the walls but the polished wood floor was bare. In her bright blue or green dress, Karin, who likes bright colors, would serve tea and cake, or homemade soup if I had arrived during the noon hour.

During our discussions throughout the year, we looked through her scrapbooks. She showed me big books filled with historic black and white photographs, notes, invitations, and newspaper clippings from the 1940s.

During the winter months, the light faded early on our conversations, and Karin illuminated the area with candlelight. The soft glow of those candles seemed to be a metaphor for the light that always surrounded her.

I learned that she had grappled with life's tough issues—a bad marriage, divorce, menial jobs, untimely deaths of loved ones—and had come through it all with a serene and loving disposition.

I was curious about her calm acceptance of things—her peace of mind. More inspirational, however, is her unselfish service to others, to the sick and suffering, the imprisoned, and the lonely.

Once, when we were standing in the entrance of NK, Stockholm's premier department store, Karin noticed that an old woman and her escort were having difficultly walking. She immediatley went to them and offered her help. They were both so grateful because the attendant could now seek extra help.

In this day and age, Karin Wiking is a phenomenon. She is a person whom you read about but never meet, yet always long to know. I call her Mother Teresa's angel in Scandinavia.

Introduction

For Swedes, Karin Wiking is a true time witness to historical events surrounding the Second World War.

As they say in the old TV news reports, "She was there." And, at 82, she is still "there." Every week, she visits a prisoner at the Stockholm jail. Daily, she's either on the phone or writing letters to one or more of 86 sick and suffering individuals—people who are registered as co-workers with Mother Teresa's Missionaries of Charity. And, weekly, she's answering the phones at Caritas, a Catholic charitable organization trying to help the world's latest victims of war, poverty and disease.

Karin Wiking is truly a woman of good will; someone who is trying to make the world a little better despite great forces to the contrary.

Current cultural elites would be attracted to Karin because of her close encounters with famous people including Mother Teresa, Pope Pius XII, Count Folke Bernadotte, French singer Maurice Chevalier, and Swedish movie star Ingrid Bergman. Without question, she has some intriguing stories to tell.

I first met Karin after moving to Sweden from McLean, Virginia, in 1994. Later, I learned Swedish Radio had interviewed her at length about her involvement in a Swedish Red Cross mission to save dying Russian POWs left in Norway by their Nazi captors in 1945.

I was fascinated. Frankly, my knowledge of World War II was not extensive. Rather than reading fact-filled historic tomes, I preferred watching old, romantic war movies. But, from Karin, I heard first-hand how the war impacted people living in Scandinavia and northern Europe.

In her early 20s, Karin worked as a Red Cross war nurse during and immediately after World War II. Her accounts of assisting the sick, wounded and starving in Finland, Norway, Germany and Czechoslovakia are memorable.

After the war, from 1946 to 1947, she worked for the United Nations in Stuttgart, Germany, assisting displaced persons stranded in Germany who longed to return to their home countries.

On one mission, she escorted 600 Poles from Germany to Poland in a series of box cars on a freight train in the middle of winter. She and one other woman, a physician, were in charge of this large group of men, women, and children for three days.

In addition, Karin recounts her experiences as a walking companion to a famous Swedish physician and author, Axel Munthe, who wrote *The Story of San Michele,* an international bestseller when it was published in 1929. Dr. Munthe, a good friend of Sweden's King Gustav V Adolf and Queen Victoria, lived at the castle in Stockholm. For 14 months, he and Karin were walking partners. At the time he was 90, and she was 27.

Since 1976, Karin has volunteered and worked for Mother Teresa in Sweden and at her Home for the Dying in India. Her stories about Mother Teresa provide an undeniable impression on the life of this extremely worthy recipient of the Nobel Peace Prize.

Finally, Karin's stories are poignant. While interviewing her one day, my tears flowed spontaneously. She was telling me about visiting a woman in the Stockholm suburbs. This lady, who "hated" her life and everyone, abruptly changed into a much nicer person during the course of Karin's visits.

Needless to say, Karin Wiking is my heroine. I hope her life touches your heart, too. Regardless of your spiritual view, she will give you fresh hope in the stormy seas of life.

Acknowledgments

I would like to thank the following people for their invaluable help on this book:

Susan Sachs, now deceased, who helped me get started and edited the first draft; Doug Cooper, who saw one of the earlier drafts of this work and offered excellent advice; Deborah Lemiska, who wonderfully edited the final manuscript; Peter Lemiska, who designed the front cover; Karl Erik Molin and his wife Berit Rönnstedt, who read an earlier draft and suggested very useful changes; Fr. Philip Geister, who suggested the interview format for this book; and, Peter Eggertz, whose support of this work was essential.

Also, I would like to thank my father, William M. Benton, and close friends, Charles Goolsby and Holly Townsend, who encouraged me to proceed with this endeavor.

I wish to deeply thank my husband, Talbot, who reviewed several drafts; and offer my love and gratitude to my family, who patiently let me work with very few interruptions. My children's support was extremely important.

In addition, I offer my everlasting appreciation to Karin Wiking, who inspired me and contributed so many messages of love and hope. She is an instrument of peace.

Lois B. Lindstrom
Stockholm, Sweden
2002

About the Interviewer

Lois Lindstrom is a freelance writer who moved with her husband and children to Stockholm, Sweden from McLean, Virgina in 1994. Her articles have been published in *The Washington Post* and *Washington Times.* She has served on U.S. Senate and Congressional staffs in Washington, D.C. A native of Richmond, Virgina, she earned her B.A. at Southern Methodist University. She resides in Sweden.

Chapter 1

Working for Mother Teresa

When did you meet Mother Teresa, one of the best-known Christians of the twentieth century?

When I first saw Mother Teresa she was speaking at Storkyrken (Stockholm's Lutheran Cathedral) in 1976, and I was in that packed church.

Did you know that she would become world famous then?

She spoke in Stockholm three years before winning the Nobel Peace Prize. I had read about her in the Catholic press, plus there had been several books written about her by then. She was becoming rather famous when I met her.

Did you find yourself drawn to her at that first encounter in Sweden?

Yes. My life has been enhanced immeasurably from my friendship with this incredible woman. She died on September 5, 1997, but her work for the "poorest of the poor" still continues every day around the world.

Many books have been written about her, and all have similar descriptions of her humility, love and resourcefulness. How would you describe her?

The power of Mother Teresa's message transcends time.

Her words at the cathedral in Stockholm were the most beautiful I have ever heard. In a firm voice she told us about her order's work by saying, "We try to bring tender love and compassion to the unwanted and unloved."

I've read that Mother Teresa had a promising career as a principal of a Bengali high school in Calcutta, India, but that she left her old order and decided to help the totally helpless in the streets. She moved to Calcutta's most miserable ghetto where she slept on the floor of a straw hut that she rented for 50 cents a month. Why did she do this?

She wanted to serve the poorest of the poor. Mother Teresa's lifestyle was based on the figure of Christ. She founded her religious order, the Missionaries of Charity, in 1950. By the 1990's, she had developed 4,600 Missionaries of Charity in 126 countries around the world—a remarkable achievement.

Why did she decide to help the poorest of the poor in the world?

I once heard Mother Teresa say that the reason for her choosing to help the poorest of the poor was love. She added, "We cannot do great things, only small things with great love." She had incredible energy and devotion.

Besides taking the usual three vows of poverty, chastity, and obedience, don't Mother Teresa's Sisters of Charity make a fourth vow, service to the poorest of the poor?

Yes.

What was her family background?

Mother Teresa was born Agnes Bojaxhiu in Albania in 1910 and grew up in a warm, Catholic family. At the age of 12, she decided to go to Calcutta after hearing letters about missionaries being read aloud at a youth club in Albania. When she was 18, she entered the Congregation of the Sisters of Loreto and left Albania for training in Ireland in 1928. She wanted to work in India and was placed in a convent there in 1929. Upon taking her final vows in 1931, she chose the name Teresa, inspired by her favorite saint, St. Teresa of Lisieux.

What did she look like? Did you see her surrounded by light or anything really unusual when you first saw her in Sweden?

I felt as if I was in the presence of a saint. Mother Teresa was so tiny that she had to stand on a box at the pulpit so those in the church pews could see her. She wore her cotton sari, bordered by three sky-blue stripes and held at the top by a clasp in the form of a crucifix, and rough leather sandals. I didn't see any special light, but there was something very spiritual about her presence.

She talked about her order's work in India in which her Sisters care for the sick and dying found on the streets of Calcutta. Mother Teresa said she and her Sisters were touching the body of Christ twenty-four hours a day when they took care of the sick and unwanted.

Did she talk about what causes all this misery and suffering?

Mother Teresa told us there was so much suffering, so much hatred, and so much misery in the world. She talked about the lack of love in the home. "All love begins at home," she said.

How did you get a chance to talk with her in Sweden? I've read that it was difficult to speak to her privately because all the Very Important People (VIPS) had secured time to speak with her at every appearance.

I knew it would be difficult to get a private meeting with her. When I read she was coming to Stockholm, I asked my Catholic priest if he could arrange a meeting with her.

After she spoke at the Stockholm lecture, I had my chance. My priest had scheduled a time for us to meet. My friends and I approached Mother Teresa by asking what we could do to help her in Sweden. She told us we should organize a co-workers group here. This co-workers group, she said, would be linked to the sisters who worked with her in India.

When we said we would love to help her, she gave me a pray card and wrote on it, "God Bless you." I still treasure that card to this day.

How did you begin to help her?

We started as a co-worker's group that met once a month. Initially, we made bandages out of old sheets and shipped them to the Missionaries of Charity in Calcutta. Mother Teresa's nuns used the bandages to cover the sores of the half million lepers who live in India. From 1977 to 1992, we shipped 20 tons of plastic sacks filled with children's clothes and bandages to her mission in Calcutta.

Didn't you use a famous prayer to open your Co-Worker meetings?

The Co-Workers of Sweden always end their meetings by saying the prayer of St. Francis of Assisi which is the expression of the concept of God acting through oneself:

"Lord, make me a channel of thy peace,
That where there is hatred, I may bring love;
That where there is wrong, I may bring the spirit of forgiveness;
That where there is discord, I may bring harmony;
That where there is error, I may bring truth;
That where there is doubt, I may bring faith;
That where there is despair, I may bring hope;
That where there are shadows, I may bring light;
Lord, grant that I may seek rather to comfort than to be comforted;
To understand rather than to be understood;
To love rather than be loved;
For it is by forgetting self that one finds;
It is by forgiving that one is forgiven;
It is by dying that one awakens to eternal life."

That prayer made us understand that God loves each person. Even if many of us are caught up in a world where everyone is striving to be richer and more powerful, God wants us to be humble and seek not to do big things, but to do small things with great love. I am a great fan of St. Francis.

How did you start the process of visiting so many sick and suffering people in Scandinavia?

Through Mother Teresa's nuns, I met Jacqueline de Decker, a nurse from Belgium. Jacqueline, who had traveled to India on her own to help the poor, met Mother Teresa in the early 1950's when she had begun similar work in the slums of Calcutta.

While in India, Jacqueline discovered she was suffering from a serious disease of the spine and had to return to Antwerp. After a period of despair, she realized that her task was to link her life of suffering and pain to the work of Mother Teresa.

Did you meet Jacqueline or just write to her?

I went to meet her in the early 1980s in Belgium. I learned that the spiritual relationship between Jacqueline and Mother Teresa was very close. Mother Teresa often said that those involved in the Sick and Suffering group were the powerhouse of the order. This praying network of people was administered by Jacqueline de Decker.

How did Jacqueline become involved as the central person for the sick and suffering?

It all began with a letter from Mother Teresa to Jacqueline in the autumn of 1952. As referenced in Kathryn Sprink's book, *A Chain of Love,* the letter began:

"Today I am going to propose something to you. You have been longing to be a missionary. Why not be spiritually bound to our society which you love so dearly. While we work in the slums, you share in the merit, the prayers and the work, with your suffering and your prayers."

This letter, for Jacqueline, brought the realization that

she was not being rejected by God but being granted instead a special role. Her task was to offer joyfully a life of suffering and pain for the work of Mother Teresa.

Jacqueline accepted the position. Recovering from what was only one of the 46 operations that she had undergone to date, Jacqueline sought among her fellow patients and sufferers those who would do the following: 1. pray for a sister in Mother Teresa's order, 2. write to that person once or twice a year, and 3. accept that their suffering would be offered in faith and love for the work of a virtual stranger in locations all over the world.

How many sick and suffering people were involved in this pray group?

As early as 1954, there were 48 Missionary Sisters of Charity linked to 48 sick and suffering people around the world ready to share in the spirit of the society and to offer their pains for a "second self." Today, there are about 4,000 Sisters and 400 Brothers.

Also, now there are more than 3,000 sick and suffering people around the world praying for the Missionaries of Charity. You realize that suffering people have been given a sense of purpose. Also, Mother Teresa's Sisters and Brothers, to whom they are linked, give them new strength and companionship in the knowledge that someone is praying for them.

How many sick and suffering people are you in contact with now (as of July 2002)?

I'm now in touch with 86 sick and suffering people in four countries: Sweden, Norway, Finland and Denmark.

What do you do for these people?

I visit them. I call and write to them; I encourage them to pray for the nuns who work at the Missionaries of Charity in Calcutta and for their missions in 126 countries throughout the world.

Who connects the sick and suffering with the specific nuns? Do you do this?

Up until several years ago, Jacqueline was the one who picked the sisters that my sick and suffering should be praying for. Now, because of extreme ill health, Jacqueline cannot continue her work so Sister Anand in Germany coordinates the sick and suffering links with the Missionary of Charity Sisters and Brothers worldwide.

What are the attitudes of the sick and suffering? Are they angry people? Is it sometimes depressing?

As a rule, the sick and suffering are easy to communicate with. This project—to pray for a nun working for Mother Teresa—gives them a purpose for their suffering. I have received some remarkable letters from my sick and suffering co-workers, who have gathered strength and a positive spirit from prayer. After our initial meeting, most of the sick and suffering are at peace and feel calm.

Have you personally used Mother Teresa's words and wisdom in talking with sick and suffering people?

Let me give you an example of someone who was not a member of the sick and suffering but was a prisoner in jail.

When I made my weekly visits to the Stockholm jail in 1999, I visited a prisoner who asked me, "How do you pray?" I told him that he should pray as it is written in the Bible (Thessalonians, Chapter 5, Verses 16-18): "When you pray, be glad, pray continuously and thank God for everything."

How did this prisoner react to those words?

He was aghast when he was told about thanking God for everything. The prisoner asked, "How can I thank God for being in jail?"

I told him to try. It is not easy. Sitting in jail in Stockholm is especially tough because of the isolation. The men and few women who are in the Stockholm jail sit in tiny cells waiting for their sentence which can take time—sometimes months.

But Sweden is very civilized. Don't the prisoners meet for exercise and meals?

The prisoners in the Stockholm jail eat in their small cells and have no one to talk with and are very isolated.

How many are sitting alone in jail right now in Stockholm?

There are at least 300 people sitting in jail in Stockholm (as of July 2002.)

What happened to the prisoner you asked to pray and be thankful for everything?

Very good news—he was able to appeal his case. He is now out of jail and back in society. He thanked God he was in jail—that was a big step for him. I told him, "Just look what happens when you change your attitude and align yourself with your creator, God. Your circumstances often change for the better."

Have you met other prisoners whose lives have been changed by prayer?

Yes. In 1994, I was making my weekly visit to the Stockholm jail and visited a 35-year-old Lebanese man, who had received a four-year prison sentence.

When I came into the cell, he was crying. When he saw I was wearing a tiny Miraculous Medal around my neck, he asked me if I was Catholic. I said yes. He asked me if I would light a few candles for him at church and pray for him, and he handed me 20 crowns (about 2 US dollars). That Sunday, I lit 10 candles for him and prayed for him.

When I returned to jail the following week, the prisoner seemed much calmer. He said he had spoken to his lawyer, and now he was optimistic. He handed me another 20 crowns and asked me to light more candles and to pray for him. That Sunday I lit another 10 candles and prayed for him.

When I went to visit him the following week, they told me he had been released from prison. He was free! I was so happy to hear that!

Did you ever see him again?

No. But I am so happy to know he had achieved freedom through the power of prayer.

Have you been to India to work with Mother Teresa?

In 1984, I traveled to India to help Mother Teresa at her mission in Calcutta.

Was it a tough trip? How long did it take?

I took a plane from Stockholm to New Delhi, India which took about 10 hours. Then, I boarded a train for the 22-hour ride to Calcutta. At the train station, I jumped into a rickshaw, but my driver couldn't find the Missionary Brother's Home in Calcutta. After spending almost an hour looking for this residence, I asked the very tired rickshaw driver to take me to the YWCA, Young Women's Christian Association.

Did you have contacts at Mother Teresa's Missionary Brother's Home?

I knew four of her Missionary Brothers who worked in Sweden, and they had suggested I use their home in Calcutta. They had told me it would be easy to find. Unfortunately, no one knew where it was. I later found the address of this residence, but I decided to remain at the YWCA.

Where did you go the next morning—to the Home for the Dying?

Actually, I traveled by rickshaw, again, to Mother Teresa's Mother House, a place where her missionary Sisters live. And, after I arrived, we all took a minibus to the Home for the Dying.

Why didn't you stay with Mother Teresa's Sisters?

Because I wasn't allowed to stay there. Mother Teresa's Sisters are not allowed to have guests.

How did India appear to you?

It appeared very poor, dirty and extremely noisy. The poor driver of my rickshaw was barefoot. As we traveled around Calcutta, I saw thousands of colorful bicycle-pulled rickshaws and, of course, dust and open sewers, chaotic and noisy traffic. For so many thousands of people in Calcutta, life is lived out on the street. Also, I was amazed to see India's holy cows roaming around in the middle of the streets, yet no one hurts them. The trains and buses were very overcrowded with people hanging out of the entrances and even clinging to the roofs. I was half expecting someone to fall off the roof of a bus. It was quite a sight! Yet, I felt so needed. I didn't feel tired. After my rickshaw driver found the YWCA, I registered for the time I would be in India and slept in a huge room divided by small partitions. There were about fifty beds in this YWCA, and one could hear everyone around them, but I slept soundly.

What did you do when you first arrived at the Home for the Dying?

The Sisters gave me an apron and a brush for the day's work. I stood in front of a big basin and scrubbed the light blue plastic mats that sick people lie on all day. I then took all the washed mats and hung them out on the roof to dry. Feeding and holding the hands of dying people, as well as dressing wounds were activities I and the other volunteers handled while working with Mother Teresa's Sisters, Brothers and helpers.

Did you worry about catching a bad germ from all these sick people?

No, because I knew I was serving God and felt I would be protected from harm. People in the Home for the Dying have every kind of disease. When I was there, they had tuberculosis (TB), asthma, and cancer, just to name a few illnesses.

Did you get emotionally close to any of the patients there?

Yes. I did care for one woman who really touched my heart. She was the youngest patient at the Home, and her name was Magdalene. She was about 30 years old and must have weighed 60 pounds. Every morning when I met her, she put her meager arms around me. She knew a little English and one day she asked, as she pointed to the spot I was standing, "Christmas, you, here?" It was December 23rd.

I immediately asked her what she wanted for Christmas.

She whispered,"Chocolates, a doll."

I promptly walked out and bought those for her that day. I also asked Sister Luke what I could give the others. She suggested buying candy. The next day I bought two boxes of typical Indian candy and distributed it to all the people in the home.

Were there any special events on Christmas Day at the Home for the Dying?

Christmas Day was very special! I helped Mother Teresa's Brothers who were organizing a Christmas feast for 400 lepers. The leper patients were sitting in long rows outside. As I passed by, I gave each one a banana leaf which they used as a dinner plate. Mother Teresa's Brothers followed me bringing rice, vegetables and sauce which they placed on the individual banana leaves.

I suppose you didn't have any silver ware?

No, we didn't. The lepers ate with their hands or stumps. Afterwards, they expressed their thanks for the meal by putting a leu of flowers around my neck. I bowed and said "Namascar" which means peace in Hindi. My leu, made of roses and lilies, was very beautiful.

I see you have many books (30) about Mother Teresa in your home. Which one is your favorite?

The famous British journalist Malcolm Muggeridge (now deceased) wrote one of my favorite books, *Something Beautiful for God,* which describes Mother Teresa's work in Calcutta. He also made a film about her work with the same name. Both have been extremely popular.

Why do you like his book so much?

His description of the work at the Home for the Dying matched mine. Let me quote from a chapter of his book: "Working at the Home for the Dying, you go through several phases. At first you feel deep sadness, mixed with pity, then you feel compassion, then you realize that these derelict men and women and these lepers with stumps for hands are the sweetest, dearest people."

That is exactly what I felt.

So the work is tough, but you were happy being there?

Strange as it might seem the atmosphere in the Home is extremely positive. The life for Mother Teresa and her Sisters was and is tough and difficult, but you really sense an atmosphere of joy. Perhaps that is why so many of the world's richest and famous people go there.

Didn't Princess Diana and John F. Kennedy, Jr. have very positive experiences visiting Mother Teresa in Calcutta?

Yes.

Describe a typical day working at the Home?

The days began with Mass at 5 a.m. After Mass, the Sisters would do the washing and other chores. Everyone had a bucket. Then came breakfast, after which, everyone went dashing off in different directions. Some go to the Home for the Dying; others go to schools and dispensaries, some to the lepers, and others look through garbage where unwanted babies are sometimes tossed.

Didn't you ever feel overwhelmed by all the poverty and disease in India?

I recalled Mother Teresa's words when she was speaking to a reporter who asked, "Haven't many people told you that what you do is just a drop in the ocean, considering the need out there?"

She replied, "Well, that drop would be missing. I'm trying to help people who can't live up to society's wants. Young people are searching for a meaning in life, and they are beginning to realize that helping others is what gives them meaning in life."

This trip to India certainly sounds as if it gave your life meaning?

It reinforced what I already knew I should be doing. It was a wonderful experience. Working with the extremely poor inspires the heart. I realized the poor in India, despite having practically nothing to eat, looked happier than most of the Swedes walking through Stockholm in the middle of winter.

Did you ever talk with any of the poor people in the streets of Calcutta?

I remember seeing this little boy, about five years old, who sat by the roadside with a sack over his shoulder glancing at a little piece of cloth in front of him, obviously for donations.

When I put some coins on the cloth, his big brown eyes still looked as sad as before. Then, I noticed a street vendor selling toys; so I bought a little toy dog that jumped and squeaked. When I put this toy on the boy's piece of cloth, a big smile slowly spread over his entire face. It made me feel so happy.

Do you know why Mother Teresa decided to organize her unique order to help the poorest of the poor?

In the beginning, Mother Teresa worked in a beautiful convent in the wealthy area of Calcutta. One day she saw a women lying in the gutter half-eaten by rats and ants. She picked up this woman and loaded her into a small cart and pushed her to the hospital, but the hospital administrators wouldn't treat her because she was so poor and ill.

How did Mother Teresa react to that negative message?

Mother Teresa didn't leave the hospital waiting room until they took the woman to be treated. She then decided that there should be some kind of home for people who were close to dying but had no where to go. After much effort on her part, the city authorities in Calcutta gave her half of the Kali Temple for her work. There were violent public protests that the city had allowed Christians to work in a public place in their city. But the mayor of Calcutta went to the protesters and said, "If your wives, your sisters and your daughters will do this work, I will tell her to leave." The protesters quietly left.

Did you ever have a chance to really talk with Mother Teresa one-on-one?

Yes. Amazingly, I did on several occasions. I had an opportunity to meet her in a private meeting in Rome. I told Mother Teresa that I had a friend with a big problem and wished she had the time to hear about it. She said, "Karin, we must talk," and she gave me an hour of her time. During this period, there was a long line of people waiting to talk with her. Despite the distractions, Mother Teresa gave me her undivided attention for 60 minutes. She has said that when someone is in front of her, that person is the only one in the world.

What was your friend's problem?

I told her that my Swedish friend's husband had been unfaithful and explained the circumstances. Mother Teresa basically said,"Your friend should forgive him. One should love the person who is cheating even more."

Do you remember the press coverage when Mother Teresa won the Nobel Peace Prize?

I recall her humble words when she was given the prize. She said, "I am unworthy of the prize. I do not want it personally. But, by this award, the Norwegian people have recognized the existence of the poor. It is on their behalf that I have come."

I still have a copy of the Norwegian daily, *Aftenposten*, which carried this editorial: "How wonderful to see the world press for once spellbound by a true star, a star without false eyelashes and makeup, without jewels and fur coats, without theatrical gestures. Her joy is the thought of spending the Nobel Prize money for the good of the poorest and most miserable of the world's people."

Did Mother Teresa ever talk about politics?

Mother Teresa was often asked by the press to comment on various wars and what she thought about them, but her usual answer was something similar to these words: "I don't understand it. We're all children of God. Nations today put too much of their effort and money into defending their borders. If they would only defend defenseless people with food, shelter and clothing, I think the world would be a much happier place." I totally agree with her.

Chapter 2

Childhood and Early Adulthood

Let's look at your early childhood. In 1920, when you were six months old, your parents left Stockholm with you and your sister and moved to Bath, England. Your father was a Brit, and your mother, a Swede. Then, after spending nine years in Bath, your family moved back to Sweden. Why?

Although my mother had great friends in England, she really missed Sweden. She actually missed the snow! After all, she was the first Swedish woman to jump from the highest ski jump in Sweden—at Fiskartorpet, on the outskirts of Stockholm in 1912. Also, she loved to skate. And, she had a very strong will. She actually convinced my father to leave his business—a gymnastics school in Bath and move back to Stockholm with her.

How did your parents meet?

They met in Stockholm when both attended the Gymnastical Central Institute, a special private gymnastics high school. (In today's terms, a junior college for Sweden's top athletes.) After graduation, my father returned to England, but he kept writing to my mother, who, after five years, had a degree as a physical therapist and was a gymnastics teacher.

During World War I, my mother worked as a physical therapist in Austria, helping wounded soldiers who had lost some of their basic motor skills. In England, my father was in charge of physical training of the British troops. In 1917, my father wrote to my mother and proposed marriage; they married in Aldershot, England, the headquarters of the British Army, where he was working at the time. Interestingly, my mother's love of adventure almost killed her. Her boat traveled from Sweden to England following some of the biggest battles of World War I, and there were still explosive mines floating in the sea.

Fortunately her ship from Sweden to the UK didn't blow up. How would you describe your parents?

My father was an extremely kind and gentle person. My mother, who was temperamental, liked having things her way. They were good parents. When we were young, they read stories to us at night. My mother actually converted the top floor of our house in England to a giant play room where we played with all our toys. My parents seemed to get along well, and both were excellent athletes.

Were they religious? Did you attend church every Sunday?

They were not so religious, and we did not attend church. My father was agnostic, but a very dear man. His sister was a Carmelite nun, and he was close to her. My mother was a Swedish Lutheran, and she made sure we were all baptized. Also, my mother taught us a simple, Swedish children's prayer, and we said a blessing at meals when we all sat together in the dining room.

Isn't there a Swedish connection on your father's side?

My father's great grandfather had immigrated to England from Värmland, Sweden in the 1800s. His son, my grandfather, maintained the Swedish connections and owned a company selling Swedish timber in London. My father embarked on another career to do what he enjoyed doing: teaching gymnastics. He moved the family from Stockholm to purchase a gymnastics training school in Bath.

While we were in Bath, my mother became pregnant with twins—a boy and a girl. As she had been pregnant every 15 months since delivering her first child, she actually had four children in three years. Fortunately, she could afford help. Because my mother's father owned a successful business (a ship building company), she was financially independent. Looking back, I think that is why my mother never learned to cook. She never had to prepare food. While we were in England, she hired a cook and two nurses to look after us.

After you moved back to Sweden, your parents took jobs teaching at a private boarding school, Viggbyholm, in a suburb north of Stockholm. You and your siblings attended school there as well. Describe your school days at Viggbyholm.

My three siblings and I joined 20 girls and 100 boys between the ages of seven and 19 at this private school. We had a nice school life, but it was an unusual one to some degree. Our headmaster, Per Sundberg, was very modern and a great idealist. He helped Jews who escaped from Nazi-Germany to become teachers and pupils at this school. Four of our teachers had escaped from Nazi Germany. Also, he told the students to call their teachers by their first names, something that is done now in Sweden, but it was quite new then. Basically, I can recall that we had fun, inventive teachers. For instance, our literature teacher, Sten Sternberg, liked taking us outdoors where we would sit and lie in the grass, and he would teach classical literature.

Do you recall the literature he discussed at the time?

Yes. He read passages from Swedish author Harry Martinsson's work, *Nässlorna Blomma.*

Did you feel like a foreigner at this school? I mean you had been raised as a Brit until you moved to Sweden. Did you feel somewhat different from the others?

My mother hired a Swedish governess to teach us Swedish one year before we left England, so I knew basic Swedish. As I had spent my life through age nine in England, I had to learn the Swedish way of looking at life. Swedes, for instance, have a reverence for truth, fair play, and respect for laws, rules and regulations. They even respect their opponents. They strongly believe in the work-together-in-teams concept. You could never boast or brag. In school, I was taught to think like a Swede. Looking back, I believe we learn patterns of behavior or ways to react to life to a much greater extent than we like to admit. I'd have to say I really enjoyed my school years. They were very pleasant.

Did you have some famous classmates who attended Viggbyholm?

One student, Rosalinde von Ossietzky, became rather famous. Her father, Carl von Ossietzky, received the Nobel

Peace Prize in 1935. He won this prestigious award because he was the editor of "Die Weltbuhne" (the "World Stage") and one of the first journalists to expose the world to Hitler's horrible atrocities toward the Jewish people. During the 1930's, the Nazis sent him to a concentration camp, and he died there.

Rosalinde was my classmate in 1935. Although she did not take the final exams at our school, she did finish high school and became a certified social worker in Sweden. Some years later, she received the Nobel monetary award on behalf of her father, who had not been allowed to leave the concentration camp to receive his prize.

Did Rosalinde contribute this prize money to Sweden somehow?

When she received the money from her father's Nobel Peace Prize, Rosalinde used it for great social purposes. She started an emergency phone line for Swedes who needed to talk to someone because they were very sad or very angry. This free social service hot line, now funded by the Swedish government, is a very beneficial social program.

Was your father happy in Sweden? Didn't your father leave the family and return to England?

When I was 13-years-old, my father was very worried about losing his school in Bath to his British partner. So he left and returned to England, but my mother refused to go with him. They didn't fight or argue; they quietly agreed to separate. They didn't divorce, and neither remarried again. When my father left, it wasn't tragic because my siblings and I sometimes visited him in England during the summers.

And, he frequently called us and always visited us at Christmas. I really think that neither one of my parents could truly emigrate from their countries. My mother was a true Swede, and my father was a true Brit!

At 19, you graduated from Viggbyholm and become the first girl at the school to take the equivalent of the college SAT's and pass them. You decided to be a social worker. At that point, you couldn't attend Stockholm's School of Social Work at Stockholm University because they required two years of practical work training before you could enter college. So, you took some interesting jobs. What was the toughest job you took and why?

Working at Ulleråker Mental Hospital, just outside of Uppsala, Sweden, was the most challenging job I undertook. I found the work quite dangerous. Tranquilizers had not yet been invented (in 1940) so we were told to watch "our backs." A mental patient could jump us from behind and try to strangle us!

You're joking. You could have been strangled?

We were always told to work in pairs. In case someone was "attacked", the other could run for help. One night, a colleague worked solo, and we, later, discovered that a patient had strangled her with a towel and pushed her under her bed. She had died.

How terrible. Were you involved in other difficult situations?

I had to stand by and watch a patient undergo electric shock therapy. It was quite terrible to witness: a patient's whole body becoming completely stiff and shaking all over.

What were some of the things you had to do at this mental hospital? You had received some basic training as a nurse, but it wasn't as if you were a registered nurse.

That's right. The first month, my friend, Gudrun Volontis, and I were assigned to work with the most neurotic patients. They were not allowed to go to the bathroom alone so we had to ask each patient to "get on the pot." Once, a patient in the women's ward whom Gudrun supervised started kicking her in the stomach as she led her to the pot. Gudrun screamed, and someone came quickly to rescue her. When a patient became violent, we had to hold him or her down and strap them down on the bed with leather belts. This took a lot of strength! We then put leather mittens on their hands.

Did you ever have a violent encounter with a patient?

I had a violent encounter with a patient one day, too. When I gave a female patient some pencils and paper for drawing, she decided she didn't want to draw. Instead, she picked up a bench and heaved it at me and the patients standing nearby! Fortunately, no one was hurt. Once, a patient threw a metal plate at me, but I ducked and didn't get hit.

I guess you were very happy to leave this job?

Actually, I thought it was very interesting. I didn't hate it.

Did you also work in a factory as a common laborer as part of your work experience to be a social worker?

Yes, as part of my two-year work experience in the real world, I also spent six months working at a large factory of 500 people in Västerås, Sweden. I was assigned to the section that made parts for bicycle lamps. I worked on the assembly line taking things off a moving conveyor belt to make a lamp part, and then placing them back on the belt for the next worker down the line to work on, and so forth.

Weren't you extremely bored with this work?

The job reminded me of the Charlie Chaplin film, "Modern Times." In that film, Chaplin works on a dehumanizing automated assembly line, and the conveyor belt goes so fast that all the products start crashing off at the end of the line. That didn't happen to us, but I learned about the difficulties of manual labor. I was very happy I didn't have to work in a factory the rest of my life.

Didn't you once tell me that X-rated material appeared on the assembly line belt?

Sometimes the girls on the assembly line put obscene drawings on the belt. When these drawings passed through, many of the girls howled with laughter, but I usually felt embarrassed.

Did the other girls working at the factory sense that you were different—far more educated and cultured than they were?

Well, at first they remarked that I spoke so eloquently. I just told them it was the "Stockholm" dialect, and they believed me.

Did you have any kind of social life after work?

In the beginning, I was so tired from the factory work, I just went to bed. But, one Saturday night I attended a town dance and met Stig Lundstam, who served in the Swedish Air Force and was an excellent dancer. We went out for several months, and he even asked me to marry him, but I turned him down as I just wasn't ready for married life. Unfortunately, he died about a year later in a plane crash.

Were you terribly sad about his death?

Yes. It was my first encounter with death. I felt very sad about Stig's untimely end.

What other work experiences did you have in your early twenties?

I received training to be a Red Cross war nurse at St. Erik's Hospital in Stockholm. There, I spent two months in the medical department, two months in the surgical department and two months in the emergency wards.

Where did the Red Cross send you on your first mission?

The Red Cross called and sent me to work at a military hospital in Gotland, that lovely island between Sweden and Finland.

While in Gotland, I became an expert at taking blood. Actually the job of taking blood is fairly easy if you are sticking the needle into a young man's arm. It's much tougher to find a vein and stick a needle into a child's arm or into a senior citizen's arm.

How long did this job last? Did you enjoy it?

This job lasted three months. As I was rather new to nursing, I had some nerve-wracking experiences. One day, the head nurse told me that one of the soldiers needed a hernia operation, and I would have to shave his groin.

Was this the first time you had ever shaved a male patient's groin?

Yes. I cautiously walked into a room filled with military men lying in their beds and found my patient. His eyes widened when I told him what we had to do; but he pulled down his pants, and I put shaving cream on his groin and started shaving.

Did you have a curtain to pull around him? Could the other men see you?

There weren't any curtains. We were out in the open. As I shaved his groin, my face turned beet red. The men, lying nearby, watching this procedure began shouting and laughing. My patient was just as mortified as I was, but somehow I got the job done and left the room without losing my composure.

Karin, you have a lot of confidence in yourself.

I suppose.

Chapter 3

War Nurse in Finland

Tell me about your first trip abroad when you worked for the Swedish Red Cross. The Second World War began in September 1939, and all the Nordic countries, including Sweden, declared neutrality. You were sent in 1942 to Finland which was then under attack by the Russians. Did Sweden assist the Finns militarily after the Russians attacked?

Sweden was not prepared to intervene militarily to help its small neighbor. Although the Swedish government was neutral, the Swedish public was very pro-Finnish. I can remember reading in Swedish publications of the period that "Finland's cause is ours." The Swedes wanted the Finns to receive our help, short of actual military intervention. I still recall seeing thousands of Finnish children arriving in Stockholm in 1942 because I worked at the Red Cross reception centers that were trying to find homes for all these children. It is not widely known that Sweden gave refuge to 36,000 Finnish children escaping the horrors of war.

Why didn't Sweden get more involved in helping Finland militarily? Was it afraid of an invasion from Germany?

Yes, it was. By early 1940, Hitler's blitzkrieg forces had invaded our Scandinavian neighbors, Denmark and Norway.

Norway and Denmark would remain under German occupation throughout the war. Historians debate whether Hitler was planning on attacking Sweden at some future date, yet I felt deep inside that Sweden would be safe from a Nazi invasion. Call it female intuition. Germany, however, did use Sweden militarily to some degree.

When Germany decided to attack Russia in June 1941, the Nazis transported a full armed division—the so-called Engelbrecht Division from Norway—through Sweden—to Finland. Did the Swedish government give Germany permission to transport troops across its territory reportedly as a way of helping Finland, now again at war with Russia?

I believe it did.

What was Sweden's Red Cross trying to accomplish in Finland?

Sweden's Prince Carl, the honorary chairman of Sweden's Red Cross at the time, had been advised there were many cases of famine in Finland—a direct result of the Soviet bombings. Concern for the Finns was rising in Sweden. I was chosen as one of six young war nurses to be flown from Stockholm to Helsinki to offer humanitarian and medical attention to the starving children in Finland.

How old were you?

I was 22.

Where did you work in Finland, and what did you do?

The Swedish nurses were assigned to work in various Finnish cities and towns. One of my colleagues, Ingeborg Söder, and I were given the task of feeding hungry children in Kotka, one of the most severely bombed cities in Finland. In fact, Soviet bombing attacks on this city were practically a daily experience for us! The actual front lines of combat between the Finns and the Russians occurred northeast of our area, but the Soviets were bombing Kotka every night because it was an important industrial center in Finland.

Were you frightened? Where did you stay in Kotka?

In the beginning, we stayed at the Swedish school in Kotka—a small, one-story wooden building. We were residing there, and we hardly slept. Russian planes dropped bombs throughout the night, each bomb making a horrible sound. The unbelievable noise made me wonder how close we were to the front lines of the fighting. One night the noise was incredibly loud. We learned that Soviet planes were dropping bombs right in our neighborhood.

You must have had a bomb shelter in the building, correct?

Unfortunately, the Swedish school where we resided didn't have a bomb shelter.

You were staying in a building without a bomb shelter, and the Russians were dropping bombs every night? Were you scared to death?

Yes. One morning, when we looked out of our window, we saw a horrible sight. All the row houses behind our house had been transformed into piles of smoldering wood framed by the remains of former chimneys. We didn't think there were going to be better times soon. It was time to leave this area.

Fortunately, a few hours later a Swedish couple came to see us and offered us their apartment in Kotka. This man and his wife were aghast that we were sojourning in a building without a bomb shelter. We would be more secure in their flat, they said, because it was in a brick building with a bomb shelter in the basement. The Swedes, who owned this flat, also owned a summer home outside of Kotka where they lived to avoid the bombing raids on the town.

How did you find the starving children and serve them food?

We had been told that we would serve food to children in a school. But the German soldiers occupied all the schools, so we had to use a simple wooden hut that served as a community center for Kotka. Inside the hut, we found a huge basin that had been used for washing clothes; however, we used it to make soup. The Swedish Red Cross supplied us with food in the form of dried soup and porridge. It was delivered from Sweden to Helsinki every couple of days and driven to our site by a Finnish volunteer.

How did the children look—really bad?

We made soup in a huge basin at this primitive community center in Kotlka. Finnish children, ages 5-12 arrived with their little buckets to get the soup. The children were so thin, all knees and elbows and wide eyes.

One little girl, about 11, with a pony tail and big blue eyes, said, "This looks delicious." Ingeborg and I just smiled and nodded as we poured the soup into her bucket. I was thinking that this was probably the first hot meal she had had in weeks, and it wasn't that great. Just vegetable broth.

Didn't you tell me once you served as an interpreter in Finland? Why?

The Germans, who were in Finland now fighting the Russians, were helping Finnish families whose homes had been destroyed by Soviet bombs. In what many would consider an unusual job for a nurse, I became the volunteer interpreter for the Germans and Finns after my work day ended, usually after six o'clock in the evening.

So not only were you a nurse, but you served as an interpreter as well?

I only did this a couple of times—not on a regular basis!

I was the German interpreter for the Finns whose houses had been ravaged by bombs and who were seeking assistance from the German soldiers. World War II history buffs may be interested to know that the German soldiers were quite helpful to the Finnish people when I was there. The German soldiers actually helped the Finns carry out to the street what was left from their burning homes. It was quite dramatic! The Germans ran into burning houses and hauled out furniture while the Finnish fire brigades tried to douse the flames.

Weren't you scared out of your wits by all the bombings?

Somehow, I didn't feel too scared, although the bombs continued to fall on Kotka. After we moved to a new residence, Ingeborg and I still had to react quickly when we heard the sirens indicating a bombing raid. We now resided in a flat on the 6th floor of a brick building in Kotka, but the elevators didn't work. When the siren sounded, which it did rather frequently at night, we had to pull on our uniforms and run down six flights of stairs to the bomb shelter in the basement.

So hearing bomb sirens going off at night became rather a routine occurrence?

You could say that. Also, we had wrap-around uniforms that were easy to put on at night in the dark. I was at my lowest weight during this period because of all the running up and down steps. Looking at my picture from this period, I was perhaps too thin, if that's possible for a woman to say anymore.

But was there ever a time that you thought you would be killed?

After a couple of weeks, we were getting used to the hear-siren-run-to-the-shelter-routine except for the night I decided not to stay in the shelter.

One day, I snapped a picture of a lovely sailing club situated on an island near the shore that I saw from my apartment window in Finland.

The following night, when we were sitting in the bomb shelter during a bombing raid, somebody called out, "the sailing club has been hit, and it's on fire!" I decided I had to see that! I could take some more photographs and have a series of shots: before, during, and after the bomb. Before taking off, I cautiously looked out the door. And, as I didn't hear any anti-aircraft firing, I decided it was safe to leave for a couple of minutes and take these pictures. After walking about 20 steps, I heard the sound of a plane above me, but as the Finnish anti-aircraft were not firing, I thought it was probably a Finnish plane.

You decided to go out while the bombs were dropping to take a picture?

I always felt I would be safe. As soon as I walked a few steps, I saw the sailing club on fire. It looked so dramatic! I wanted to get closer and take that prize-winning picture, even though I had a very inexpensive camera.

As I walked toward the harbor, I heard the whistling sound of a bomb hurling close by. When it struck the ground about 50 meters away from me, I was physically thrown back by the bomb's impact.

Whew, I thought, this is getting too close for comfort. I wasn't hurt, thank goodness, but I was really frightened. Luckily, I saw two men running ahead of me.

You must have been happy to see those men? Did you yell for help?

I sure did. I ran after them. "Let me go with you," I yelled to them. They heard my yelling and slowed down long enough so I could join them as we rushed to the nearest bomb shelter in the harbor area.

They must have been surprised to see you, a young woman taking a walk on such a night?

These men were Finns, and they didn't look glad to see me.

"What were you doing out there?" one of the men asked me in an angry tone.

"I was taking pictures," I admitted, feeling a little embarrassed.

The two men looked at me as if I were crazy. Then, they both took me by each elbow, and we ran to the bomb shelter. While we were in the shelter, we met two Finnish sailors. They told us one of their mates had had his head cut off by shrapnel from a bomb that had been dropped nearby. They also said the Soviet plane dropping bombs had been flying too high for the anti-aircraft guns to hit it.

Did it now dawn on you that you could have been killed?

I was shocked! I realized I might have been killed! It was the first time I had contemplated such a thought since arriving in Finland.

How did your roommate, Ingeborg, react to your picture-taking episode?

Several hours later, I returned to my residence and ran into Ingeborg, who was furious.

"Are you crazy?" she asked. "What would I have said to your mother if you had died? I promised your mother I would look after you, but you're making it very difficult!"

"I'm so sorry Ingeborg. I won't do that again," I said, feeling very apologetic.

Ingeborg, who was five years older than I, just shrugged her shoulders and became silent. She had promised my mother she would look after me. Unfortunately, she never really got over the fact that I left the building without telling her during that bombing attack.

Did you have other Red Cross missions in Finland?

Before we returned to Stockholm, Ingeborg and I traveled to Vyborg to help the other Swedish nurses who were stationed there. Vyborg, a town east of Kotka, had been almost totally destroyed.

Following that exciting introduction to Red Cross nursing, didn't you start working for the British Embassy? How did you get that job?

When I returned to Stockholm, I received a letter from the British Red Cross. I don't know how they discovered that I had a British passport and was half British. The British Red Cross asked me to join their organization in England. It was 1943, and World War II dominated our lives. I thought serving in the British Red Cross would be very exciting, so I made plans to move to London.

However, God works in mysterious ways. A British courier plane leaving Stockholm for England was shot down by the Germans. The British decided to wait a while before sending more courier planes to England from Sweden. Meanwhile, the British government asked me to work for them at the British Embassy in Stockholm. I accepted that position and worked as a confidential archivist from 1943-1945. I filed secret papers for the British government, pledging never to divulge what I saw. To this day, I've honored that pledge.

Did the Swedish government sell weapons to the Germans?

I can't comment.

Why not? It's been so many years since the Second World War?

I signed a letter stating that I would never disclose what I saw while working at the British Embassy, and I keep my promises.

Didn't you become engaged to be married to a man who worked at the British Embassy?

Yes, I fell in love with Bill Varley, who was assigned to the British Embassy in Stockholm on a special assignment. He was supposed to return to England, but he didn't because we were in love. He extended his stay in Sweden; we became engaged, and our relationship lasted about six months. Bill was an archeologist and a former professor at Christ Church University in England. However, there was a major problem with our relationship—he was fifteen years older than I. I ended the relationship because he was just too old. I was 23 and not quite ready for married life.

How did you break up with him? Was he angry?

He had been transferred back to the U.K, so I just wrote him a letter saying my plans to marry him had changed.

Did he write back to you?

The funny thing is, he probably did, but I don't remember.

Chapter 4

War Nurse in Norway

You were on a Swedish Red Cross humanitarian mission to Norway in June 1945. On this trip 31 Swedes traveled to Fauske, Norway, about 100 kilometers above the Arctic Circle, to save former Russian prisoners of war (POW's) who had been brutalized by their Nazi captors. Weren't the Russians concerned about their military men who reportedly were starving to death?

Red Cross headquarters in Stockholm had received word that former Russian POWs had been left to starve in Norway. Neither the German Nazis nor the Russian Communists cared what happened to them. There were also reports of TB and other illnesses among the 30,000 Russian troops left in prison camps near Fauske, Norway. As many as 80,000 Russians had originally been working in forced labor camps in Norway, but because of the severe lack of food, untreated illnesses and extreme cold, some 50,000 died.

I have read articles in Swedish newspapers about this mission. Did reporters interview you? How many doctors were in the group?

When our Swedish Red Cross team of doctors and nurses arrived in Fauske, Norway, we received a lot of press attention. Although I wasn't interviewed, pictures of our group were in the papers, as well as stories about this mission. There were six doctors, along with five other war nurses, including me, and six regular nurses, plus cooks and Russian translators assigned to this mission.

What did you find when you arrived in Fauske, Norway?

We saw a very simple field hospital that had 350 beds. The first night was really hard. The Nazis had stuffed rags in the pipes, so we didn't have any water. Plus, there were huge rats as big as cats roaming the halls of the hospital because of all the trash on the floors.

In those terrible conditions, we gave three full meals and administered medicine to the starving men. And, while the three cooks prepared the food, we were able to clean this hospital.

At first, the Russians could eat very little because they were so close to starvation. Seventeen men died the first night we arrived. But as we began feeding them, they started to regain their health.

I suppose the Russians were extremely thin?

They were shockingly thin! The Russian soldiers, actually POWs, had been left to die in Norway. They told us they survived on one piece of bread and watery soup given to them daily during the war. You must remember they had been working and living in freezing cold conditions for months at a time building railways and roads for the Nazis.

What else did you do for them besides give them food?

We checked each man's medical condition. We took temperatures, gave medicine, and changed bed pots. Since many of the men were bedridden, we had to change pots quite frequently. We also had several containers of disinfectant that we used to clean every millimeter of the field hospital.

What did you do when someone died?

Whenever someone died, two Russian helpers hauled him away, and another sick Russian quickly took the empty bed.

What did you do to relax in these horrible circumstances?

We learned Russian.

You learned Russian to relax? Do you still know any Russian words?

We only learned simple sentences. For instance, I learned how to ask the Russian patients about their families. They were so moved that we tried to communicate in Russian that tears rolled down their cheeks. No one had spoken Russian to them since they were taken to Norway.

Could you understand a Russian if he told you about his family?

Not really. We nurses smiled a lot as we really didn't understand too much Russian. I knew phrases like "Thank You" and "How are you?" And, we knew the Russian words for good and bad. I remember the Swedish nurses really liked hearing the Russian word, "Horashó" which means good.

How was the weather in Norway? Could you go for walks?

Actually, the time we spent in Norway was memorable both for the sunny weather, and the nice camaraderie of the Swedish medical team.

At meal time, we sat outside at a big wooden table, and the view was spectacular. The Norwegian countryside was bathed in sunlight; we were surrounded by snow capped mountains; and the temperature stayed above 20 Celsius (73 F). Wild flowers were in bloom all around us, and we ate familiar Swedish food that we had brought from Stockholm.

It almost sounds like a scene from a film. Were you eating in sunlight at 10 o'clock at night?

Yes, we were dining late. When we ate together late at night (with the sun still shining), one of the Swedish doctors often played his guitar, and we sang Swedish songs. The Russians were shocked to see both doctors and nurses coexist as equals. Not only did we all eat together, but we all worked as a team unloading the supplies from the small military plane that arrived once a week from Sweden.

Why were the Russians so concerned about doctors and nurses eating and working together?

Although Russian Communist members promoted egalitarianism, the reality was separatism. The Russians, we learned, received benefits and perks based on their title and position, and the Russian nurses ranked far below the Russian doctors in the social hierarchy.

The Swedes, on the other hand, have practiced egalitarianism since the 1920's. Then, as today, we are automatically on a first-name basis with one another, regardless of age, sex, social position or job title. Sweden doesn't have a top-down ruling class so everyone is considered capable, and we all strive for consensus and harmony.

Didn't you have a problem with Soviet KGB agents at the hospital?

Soviet government secret agents appeared on the scene within days of the convoy's arrival. We were trying to help these dying Russians, and this Soviet agent kept telling them not to trust us. We were labeled "capitalistic Swedes."

What did the Soviet agents do? Did they go around whispering in patients' ears not to trust the Swedes?

Not exactly. One of the agents came regularly to the hospital to give speeches. He would walk into each of the five patient rooms and in a booming voice give a propaganda speech about the evils of capitalistic Sweden.

How did the Swedish doctors and nurses react to those diatribes?

We ignored the Russian agent and his speeches.

Were there any areas where the Swedish doctors and nurses and the Russian military worked well together?

Interestingly, patriotic gestures became matters of infinite importance. The Russians created a sickle and hammer flag using pebbles and rocks in front of the field hospital. The Swedes sat down on the ground at the same time as the Russians and created their own flag from pebbles and rocks on other side of the hospital's entrance.

"Which flag looks the best?" I asked to Ingrid, another Swedish nurse.

"Ours does," she replied, adding, "at least we designed both of them in the spirit of friendship."

You told me that you really liked one of the Russians who arrived in Norway from Moscow. What was he like?

One of the Russians, who was a medical student and had arrived with 10 other Russians, developed a crush on me. This Russian, Alexej Borisov, 24, gave me a beautiful wooden box he made during his stay in Norway. I still have the box and treasure it to this day! Alexej was assigned the tough job of lifting all the heavy boxes and cleaning the floors so I saw him around the hospital quite frequently. I really liked him, but I would say he fell in love with me.

When I was about to leave Norway to return to Sweden, Alexej gave me a bucket of wild flowers. Tucked inside was a love poem written by the Russian poet, Nekrasov, entitled, "Adoration." I still have that poem. It translates:

"I am captivated, I am enchanted,
By you, of whom I couldn't take my eyes off.
I am for centuries bound to you
With a chain of fatal love

I am your slave, my sovereign
Everything I bring forth to your feet.
Without you the world is a prison.
Alas, believe my words

Your lively eyes, your little hand,
Your foot, your curls,
Your body, I will remember
Day and night
Full of passion like a volcano

I beg you cast a glance on the sufferer,
Even if by a mistake, and grant me
At least once a friendly smile.
I love you, don't ridicule me.
I ask you to love me
When you have the inclination
I will live only for you."

That poem seems to express the passion of the Russian soul. How did you get along with him? Did you like his romantic overtures?

When Alexej wrote his name and address in my diary, a Soviet agent appeared and smudged out his address. The agents were very concerned that we would try to communicate, and that I might entice him to join me in Sweden.

When did you have a chance to be with Alexej privately?

On my birthday! My birthday falls on June 24 and in 1945, I celebrated it in Fauske, Norway. The Norwegians traditionally celebrate Midsummer's Eve on the 23rd of June, and they observe the holiday by lighting bonfires on their mountains tops.

Alexej and I, and other friends, walked to the top of one of the hills near Fauske and saw these beautiful bonfires on the gorgeous surrounding mountaintops. It was like a dream because it was quiet and peaceful; and, the midnight sun shone and all the Russians sang songs. The sun never went below the horizon. After midnight, it started to slowly rise again, and that's when the Russians earnestly began celebrating my birthday.

The Russians formed a circle around me and began singing the Russian song, "Katja Katjuschka." They called me Sister Katja. Katja is the Russian interpretation of Karin.

That night, Alexej leaned over and kissed me. It was a very innocent kiss, and it felt like a beautiful drop of rain. We didn't do anything more than that. I thought he was so sweet and kind.

The Russians have a reputation for being very passionate. Did any Russian patients show a romantic interest in you and the other nurses?

Not that I can remember. The Russians struck me as a very impassioned people in both their poems and their songs. Once, when I walked into one of the large hospital rooms, I heard beautiful music. These very sick men lying on cots were singing hauntingly melodic Russian songs. Their voices joined in perfect harmony. They actually sounded like a professional choir as they sang a rousing Russian army drinking song. Many of them were dying, but their outstanding vocal ability belied that fact.

Didn't you also have a very scary encounter with some German soldiers who were still camped near your hospital?

The departing German Army had a big camp less than a

mile from our field hospital. They still had their weapons, and we often heard drunken Germans singing at night. My co-nurses and I were forbidden to walk alone on the roads, day or night, because the German army had not left the area.

Early one morning, a German soldier opened the door of our quarters (a small wooden house near the hospital) and just stood there staring. Twelve of us (Swedish nurses) were sleeping in one room, in bunk beds. When I woke up and saw this soldier, I really thought we might be raped because I wasn't sure if there were more Germans right behind him, just outside the door. It was scary!

Did you scream? What did you do?

One of the Swedish nurses, sat up in her bed, and hollered in her best French,"Ferme la Porte!" (Close the Door!) The soldier abruptly left. We were so relieved.

What happened when the Swedish team left Fauske?

After a month in Fauske, the Swedish Red Cross team returned to Stockholm. And, the Russians arrived by boat to take their men back to Russia.

Did the Russians take their men back to Russia?

As we were leaving, I felt emotionally heartsick. It was an incredibly dramatic exit! The thin, Russian patients were lying in beds in our field hospital with tears streaming down their faces as we said good bye and walked out with our suitcases and supplies.

Why were they so sad? Had the Russians fallen in love

with the Swedish nurses?

Our Russian/Swedish interpreters told us the Russian men were afraid to return to Russia. They said Stalin told his soldiers to save the last bullet and to never be captured. In other words, Russian soldiers had been told to commit suicide rather than be taken prisoner. I could not bear to think that these POWs might be going to another prison in Siberia or be shot as traitors. I felt so sad for Alexej.

Did you ever see Alexej again?

Unfortunately, I never saw him again. After I returned to Stockholm, Alexej sent me a letter through a Norwegian volunteer. I never replied. I thought it was too dangerous for him to be in contact with someone from the West.

Chapter 5

White Buses in Germany

Count Folke Bernadotte, a grandson of Oscar II, King of Sweden and Norway, was one of the most admired Swedes during World War II. In 1942, he was Vice Chairman of the Swedish Red Cross. Because his uncle, 83-year-old Prince Carl was the Chairman, Count Bernadotte, in practice, became head of the Red Cross. Under his leadership, Sweden's Red Cross provided relief expeditions saving Jews and Scandinavians captured by Hitler's Third Reich. You were involved in some of those missions. Can you describe what happened? And how many people did he save?

Count Bernadotte's expeditions saved about 30,000 concentration camp prisoners and brought them to freedom in Sweden. In some of these missions, he took serious personal risks. For example, his jeep was almost hit twice by shrapnel from Allied bombing during a mission in Germany in March of 1945. Also, he negotiated with famous Nazis such as Heinrich Himmler, Head of the Gestapo and Minister of the Interior, and passed Himmler's surrender offer to the Allied powers.

Were you involved in the early 1945 Swedish Red Cross missions?

No, I didn't participate in those missions. However, I was involved in a mission to Germany in September of 1945, after the conclusion of the war.

When you first met Count Bernadotte, what was your impression of him?

I first met Count Bernadotte in Norway when I traveled with the Swedish Red Cross to Fauske to help former Russian POWs. I accompanied the Red Cross Vice Chairman in a jeep from our field hospital in Fauske to a nearby primitive looking airfield.

During this trip, he asked me why I became a Red Cross war nurse.

"I enjoy this work," I told him. "I like helping people."

He said he liked helping people, too, and then he became silent and appeared deep in thought for the rest of the journey. He was handsome, carried himself with dignity, and spoke persuasively.

Were you attracted to him? Did you have long conversations?

Count Bernadotte did not make idle conversation. I know he felt very keenly about the importance of helping the less fortunate. He was also very happily married, so I didn't have a romantic interest in him.

Why was he so interested in helping the less fortunate?

Perhaps it was the influence of our religion. Both of us were members of the Lutheran Church which in the 1940s was the state religion of Sweden. Out of seven million Swedes in the 1940s, 90 percent were members of the Lutheran Church.

When I was a student, all of the schools in Sweden were under the influence of the church. We were taught the importance of helping the less fortunate, which I believe was stressed a great deal more than in schools today. The fact that Count Bernadotte undertook his Red Cross position with such whole-hearted dedication and enthusiasm impressed me.

When did you actually go on a mission with Count Bernadotte?

Following our meeting in Norway, I met Count Bernadotte again when I was recruited as one of 28 people to serve on a Swedish Red Cross mission to Germany between September 30 and December 2, 1945. We traveled in three buses painted white and one truck. Actually, Count Bernadotte did not travel with us but stayed at the Red Cross headquarters in Lubeck. We were on a humanitarian mission and did not have a big budget for accommodations.

Where did you sleep?

We slept in a big military tent-all 20 men and four women. A small stove in the middle of the tent provided heat, but it wasn't too efficient. When we slept in our sleeping bags, our heads were cold, but our feet were hot because they were nearest the stove. Everyone behaved with restraint and decorum, and no one left their sleeping bags at night.

Who did you rescue on this trip to Germany?

Our first stop was the Nazi Concentration Camp at Bergen-Belsen. Our task was to take Polish Jews from this dreadful concentration camp to the Danish border.

That must have left an indelible impression, did it not?

It certainly did. When we arrived at Bergen-Belsen, I saw the ovens and mass graves where thousands of Jews had been killed and buried. I actually saw an area by the incinerators piled high with shoes that once belonged to children and adults who had been burned to ashes. Shocked and disgusted, I almost became physically ill.

I remember asking a German man who was standing nearby, "Didn't you know what was going on?"

"No!" he replied and quickly walked away. But, I didn't believe him. The citizens in the town near this concentration camp must have known what was happening. They must have smelled the burning human flesh and seen the smoke that drifted up and over the town. With my inexpensive camera, I documented the horrors of this place by photographing the mass graves and various signs placed throughout the camps.

Describe one of your photographs?

I photographed the infamous Bergen-Belsen Concentration Camp sign on which is written: "Liberated by the British April 15, 1945, 10,000 unburied dead found here. Another 13,000 have since died. All were victims of the German New Order in Europe and an example of Nazi Culture."

How long did you stay at Bergen-Belsen? Where did you go after that camp?

Fortunately, we did not stay long at Bergen-Belsen. The white buses left for the Danish border with the former Jewish inmates as passengers. In Denmark, they were to be checked for disease and lice, and other medical problems before traveling to Sweden.

For three months, we traveled by bus to various locations in Germany picking up "displaced people" and taking them to other locations. Once, our bus picked up some Swedish women and children who had been left by their now deceased or imprisoned German husbands and fathers. We took them to Denmark and from there they made their way to Sweden.

Do you remember any other exciting incidents during these missions?

One day, while I was at the Red Cross headquarters in Lubeck, Germany, Count Bernadotte drove up with German Princess Marie Elizabeth of Wied. He told me that his passenger, the princess, was sick with the flu. Count Bernadotte then asked me if I would be her nurse, and I immediately said yes. I really enjoyed the princess's company, and we became very good friends.

Describe Princess Marie Elizabeth of Wied.

Princess Marie Elizabeth was nicknamed "Malibeth." She was 27, and she spoke Swedish. Her father had served as the German Envoy to Sweden during World War II, and that is why she knew my language. Both of her parents and her sister were imprisoned shortly after the war because of their Nazi affiliation, but Malibeth had been found innocent. After she recovered from the flu, she returned to Sweden.

Didn't Swedish Queen Louise practically adopt Malibeth as her own daughter?

In Stockholm, Malibeth met Queen Louise of Sweden. The queen, who did not have any children of her own, really liked Malibeth and treated her very well, as a family member.

After I moved back to Sweden permanently in 1947, Malibeth invited me to a very nice party at her apartment in Fredhäll, a part of Stockholm. Queen Louise had provided Malibeth with a lovely apartment and gave her spending money. The Swedish queen liked her so much that when she died, she left Malibeth quite a large sum of money.

How did you like Malibeth's party? It must have been very glamorous?

It was really fun! My date was an Englishman, Roland Goodall, whom I had met in the summer of 1947 at the Royal Tennis Club in Stockholm. Tall and handsome, with blue eyes and wavy brown hair, Roland was very appealing. At the party, Malibeth and Roland talked quite a bit. Roland and I were just good friends and not romantically involved, so I was delighted that Malibeth liked him.

Did your friend, Roland, and Malibeth begin dating?

In fact, Roland started giving Malibeth English lessons every week. But Queen Louise didn't think an English officer was suitable to be Malibeth's husband. Poor Roland, who longed to be with Malibeth, did not get his residency permit approved to stay in Sweden. I think the queen wanted him to leave and stop his romantic pursuit of her beloved princess.

Did Malibeth ever marry?

Interestingly, Malibeth never married. She became a writer of children's books. I still have her autographed copy of *Lilltrollet,* a book she wrote about Princess Christina of Sweden. In all, she wrote four books and led a very productive life, but that is another story.

After your trip to Germany, Count Bernadotte was appointed the United Nations mediator in Palestine on May 20, 1948. He became the first official mediator in the history of the UN. While in Palestine, he succeeded in achieving a truce in the first Palestinian war between the Jews and the Arabs and laid the groundwork for the UN relief organization for Palestine refugees. Did you see him again after he took this new job?

In 1948, he made his one last visit to Stockholm as the Chairman of the International Red Cross Conference. I was appointed the "attache" for the Spanish delegation and took off from my SAS job to work at this conference for one weekend. At the conference, I saw Count Bernadotte, who gave me an official portrait photograph which he autographed.

Did you know his wife well?

No. But I received a very nice letter from her when I sent her a photograph of her and her husband together just before he boarded a plane for Palestine, at the Stockholm International Airport near Bromma. I believe this photograph meant a lot to her.

Count Folke Bernadotte was killed by Jewish extremists

on September 17, 1948, a few days before he was scheduled to present a proposed political plan on the Palestinian question to the UN. Were you involved in his funeral procession in Sweden?

Yes. His body was flown back to Stockholm and his funeral procession was watched by thousands of Swedes. My good friend, Hilla Brita Thott, and I walked behind his casket carrying the Red Cross flags, along with about 30 others who had served in the Red Cross with him. To commemorate his life and death, memorial services were held all over the world.

Did they ever find the extremists who killed him?

No, they did not.

Chapter 6

White Buses in Czechoslovakia

I recall one of your most exciting Red Cross trips took place in Czechoslovakia in the winter of 1946. What happened?

Between January 3, 1946 and February 3, 1946, I traveled to Pilsen, Czechoslovakia from Lubeck, Germany in one of Count Bernadotte's white buses. Our mission was to rescue 123 Sudeten German prisoners in Czechoslovakia.

Who were the Sudetens?

They were Germans who lived in Sudetenland—a border area between Czechoslovakia and Germany.

It was the Sudetenland, then a section of Czechoslovakia, which Edvard Benes, the former Czech president, had been told he must surrender to Hitler's government in 1938. Its loss to Hitler was regarded as a peaceful gesture, not appeasement to a dictator.

Is this the land in Czechoslovakia that British Prime Minister Neville Chamberlain agreed to let Hitler have in September of 1938, and then proclaimed he had achieved "peace with honor," and that, as a thankful result, everyone should "go home and get a nice sleep."

Yes. Unfortunately, for the residents of Sudetenland and for all Europeans, I included, a peaceful sleep was impossible until Hitler's forces finally surrendered in May of 1945.

How many Swedish Red Cross buses were involved in this mission? How many Sudeten Germans were you expecting to rescue?

Our convoy to Pilsen included 13 buses, many filled with sacks of clothes and containers of food donated to the Swedish Red Cross. We were picking up the 123 Sudetens from a prison camp called Camp Karlov, and taking them to Helsingborg, Sweden where they would be resettled in various towns and cities in Sweden. Twenty of the group were children, but it wasn't as grim as visiting the concentration camp in Bergen-Belsen. Although the Sudetens were thin, they were in reasonably good health.

Were these prisoners in a concentration camp?

They were in a former Nazi concentration camp, now in the hands of the Czech government. And, these prisoners were guarded by Czech soldiers. This camp had a series of low level wooden buildings, former barracks. I remember the area outside where the Sudetens were housed was covered with snow and ice. The old wooden building where they stayed had one light— a light bulb hanging from the ceiling in the center of the room. There wasn't any heat so everyone huddled together to keep warm. Some of the former prisoners were holding little sacks with everything they now possessed. It smelled awful because they hadn't been able to bath properly for quite some time.

I suppose the scene at the window of your bus looked very desolate. Do you remember any scenes from that trip?

One vision remains: seeing the flattened, bombed-to-smithereens town of Lidice. Apparently the Czechs partisans shot a very senior German officer, Reinhard Heydrich, who had been head of the Gestapo in 1942. In revenge for his death, the Nazis bombed the entire town of Lidice out of existence. The original population of Lidice was 10,000. The town's population when our bus drove by: 0.

Did the Nazis kill everyone in the town including women and children?

I later learned that the Nazis took the women and children from Lidice to concentration camps and left the Czech men there before bombing the town. I still have the photo I took from our bus window as we passed by this flattened town.

I recall you mentioned extremely icy conditions. Didn't one of the Red Cross buses skid on the ice and flip over? Was anyone hurt?

While traveling to Prague from Pilsen, Czechoslovakia, the white bus I was in skidded on the ice and flipped over, horizontally across the highway, blocking all traffic lanes.

It's a day I shall never forget. I was the only woman and one of four people in that overturned bus. Hilla Brita Thott, the other Red Cross nurse from Sweden, sat in a bus behind ours. Fortunately, I was sitting next to Detlow von Braun, a strong Swede who held onto me when our bus flipped over. I was barely bruised, thanks to Detlow, who had protected me with his massive body.

It's incredible no one was hurt.

It truly was. We all crawled out of the back door of the bus, and everyone said they were "ok." It surprised me no one had been hurt. The force of the bus skidding out of control, hitting a stone pillar, and flipping over, knocked the spare tire off the back of the bus. It landed some distance away in the woods.

Had your bus driver warned everyone so people should get prepared for a potential accident?

Moments before our bus flipped over, the bus driver, a 19-year-old Swede named Sigge, had shouted, "I can't handle this, any longer." His yelling woke up the other bus driver, who was sleeping on the top of sacks of clothes in the back of the bus. When he heard Sigge shout, he jumped off the sacks and sat down in a bus seat and hung on. He might have been seriously hurt if he had stayed asleep on top of those clothes bags when our bus flipped over.

What happened next? Were the other buses in your convoy assisting you?

After I crawled out of the bus, Hilla Brita ran up to me, and we gave each other a quick hug. But there wasn't time to commiserate; the man in charge told us to start redirecting traffic so there wouldn't be any more accidents. Since our bus had landed across the highway, and there were many vehicles approaching the site, we wanted to prevent a massive pile-up.

As I was weighing our chances of being stranded in this blizzard, the Czech military arrived. A group of soldiers actually pushed our bus into its upright position. Their physical strength was incredible! All the windows on our bus had shattered, but mechanically the bus was fine. Then Sigge, our driver, jumped back into the driver's seat, we passengers boarded the bus, and we drove to our destination. Despite the awful weather and poor driving conditions, we even took the time to fetch the spare tire that had flown into the woods. It was a pretty cold ride since all the windows were gone, and the wind draft blew the snow inside the bus.

I imagine you were ready for bed that evening. Any other dramatic events on this trip?

We arrived in Prague ready to collapse after that stressful day. Several days later, we boarded the buses to visit another prison camp in Czechoslovakia. On that trip, Percy Norling, a Swede, drove the supply truck, in front of our bus.

Then an amazing thing happened! As our bus approached a railroad crossing, we saw a train coming at full speed. Percy, driving the truck ahead of us, apparently didn't see the train, and he didn't stop his truck. Then the most awful thing happened. One of the railway poles at the crossing slammed down on the front window of his truck and the other pole hit the back of his truck, causing it to stall on the tracks, just as the train was approaching.

Did everyone on your bus scream in horror?

I think we were silent—in shock. In what I call a miracle, the engineer managed to stop the train brakes just in the knick of time. The sound of screeching brakes was incredible! Poor Percy had a big cut on his face. When the first railway pole hit his truck, it had smashed the window, and the shattered glass cut his face.

Did you get a picture of this amazing scene? I suppose you were too caught up in the drama of the event to take a picture?

I desperately wanted to take a picture of this incident because it was so amazing to see the train within an arm's length of the stalled truck on the tracks. But, I had more pressing business and couldn't take that prize winning shot. I had to take care of Percy. I jumped off the bus and went over to him with my Red Cross bag to fix his cut. He smiled bravely when he saw me! Afterward, we took Percy to a nearby hospital to have his face wound stitched because the bandages would not be enough.

How did you and your friend, Hilla Brita, cope with the stress of this job?

The trip through Czechoslovakia ended nicely in Prague. We went dancing with some very good looking Swedish officers that same evening. Also, adding to my positive memories of this adventure was the companionship of my good friend, Countess Hilla Brita Thott.

Hilla Brita and I remained friends for more than 50 years. She married a Swedish count and while they were on their honeymoon cruise to South America, he became ill and died. The cruise ship's captain buried her husband at sea. Hilla then moved to Madrid and never married again. We kept in touch through calls, letters and visits. She moved to Lund, Sweden in her 70's and died in 1997.

Chapter 7

Displaced Persons

On March 6, 1946, you received a new job. You were assigned to the United Nations Relief and Rehabilitation Administration (UNRRA) in Arolsen, Germany. This was an administrative processing center for survivors of the war, or displaced persons, many of whom were in a stateless and penniless condition. Can you describe your work environment there?

Our headquarters were located in two ornate, monumental German palaces that had been seized by Allied Forces during the war. Inside the first castle was a massive group of offices that had been turned into a large administrative center for the UNRRA offices. This is where I worked.

What about the other castle? Was it in close proximity to the one used for administrative purposes? How was it used?

The first castle, where I worked, had been converted into offices. Inside the second castle (within a quick walk nearby) was really an impressive site. The massive front door opened into a lovely foyer. Its interior was decorated with beautiful statues and turn-of-the century frescoes. Beyond that spread a huge room with a beautiful marble floor and hanging above was a gorgeous chandelier suspended from the high ceiling.

The walls were covered in Italian marble and the grand staircase was wide enough for eight people to ascend at once.

Didn't you tell me the staff used this castle for social events such as dances?

Yes, they did. This castle had two dream-like ballrooms on the first and second floors. Both were lined with mirrored walls and gold painted pillars. Every Saturday night UN staff members, myself included, danced to gypsy music in the ballroom on the top floor and American pop music in the ground floor ballroom. Needless to say, the UN staff in Arolsen had a wonderful social life.

How many people were at these dances?

I would imagine there must have been almost 100 people there.

Besides dancing at night and working during the day, you took tea with two teenage German princesses who lived in the attic of one of these castles. Where were the princesses' parents?

When the UN staff first arrived in Arolsen, they found two German princesses living in one of the castles. Unfortunately, their parents had been arrested and imprisoned because they were Nazis. However, their teenage daughters, Margareta, 17, and Ingrid, 14, were allowed to continue living in their home, albeit in the attic, along with the United Nations staff and administrative offices.

Margareta and Ingrid were nice, polite girls. For two months, I taught them English on a daily basis. We usually had tea together in the late afternoon which was rather pleasant.

When did you start working with destitute refugees?

Although I liked my work at headquarters, I longed to do more to assist the refugees. I wanted to help the "displaced persons" who had been placed in resettlement camps throughout Germany. So I applied for such a position at the UN in Stuttgart. After filing the appropriate work forms and telling anyone in charge of my intentions, I finally succeeded in getting a new job—at the UN Relief and Rehabilitation Administration (UNRRA) in Stuttgart.

Soon after, I was assigned to assist in the repatriation of displaced Poles living in Germany. Altogether, 600 Poles—former POWs and civilian inmates including men, women and children— were repatriated back to Poland. During the war, they were in Nazi concentration camps and prisons. But, when the war ended in May 1945, they were placed in resettlement camps throughout Germany.

I understand you began the repatriation of 600 people in December 1946 on a train journey that began in Stuttgart and ended at the Polish border. Describe this trip.

It was a difficult journey, both emotionally and physically. There were only two of us in charge—my colleague, Dr. Hedda Klepetar, a Czech medical doctor, and I. Since we didn't have visas to enter Poland, now administratively in the hands of the Russians, we were only able to accompany the refugees to the Polish border.

Were you traveling on a passenger train?

No! We traveled in twenty boxcars hooked to a freight train during that cold December. There were about 30 refugees in each boxcar. Crossing the devastated, former war zone in boxcars in the middle of winter was exhausting. Traveling in a boxcar of a freight train is a far cry from a passenger train. It was a big job for two people—myself and Hedda, who was Jewish, to supervise this group of 600 bedraggled persons in 20 boxcars. The train ride was noisy, smelly, and cold. Hedda took charge of anything that required medical attention. I was in charge of heating and distributing food and water to our passengers.

What did you have to eat?

We ate American K rations and used portable stoves in each of the 20 boxcars. The stoves were placed in the middle of each train car for heating food, and each stove had pipes that were made out of metal that jutted out of an open door of each boxcar.

Did you have to visit each boxcar to deliver the food three times a day?

No, fortunately. When the train stopped, which it did every couple of hours so people could physically relieve themselves, several people from each boxcar came over to me to get the food for that particular meal-breakfast, lunch, or dinner.

How did you handle the problem of privacy with people using the great outdoors to relieve themselves?

There were doors on both sides of the boxcars, so the women and girls jumped off on one side of the car and the men and boys jumped off the other when we made "pit stops." As we were traveling in December, this three-day journey was very cold and uncomfortable.

Did your passengers get along? Did anyone get very sick?

Fortunately, everyone was cooperative. Luckily, no one became very sick or gave birth to a baby. Also, there were 10 American soldiers aboard this train who walked around guarding it. I learned that this very same train had been attacked by starving Germans the last time it had crossed the eastern part of Germany.

Did these American soldiers make you feel more secure?

They sure did! Also, they were a big help in getting the heavy boxes opened which contained all the food packets for these 600 people.

You once mentioned that you saw many Communist propaganda signs as you approached Poland? What did you and Dr. Klepetar do as the train approached the Polish border?

As our train approached the Polish border, we saw Communist propaganda signs everywhere. Our train stopped right before the border between Germany and Poland, and our passengers left us to walk across the border into Poland. We jumped off the train to say, "Goodbye and good luck." Later, Hedda and I were picked up at the German/Polish border by an UNRRA official in a jeep. Next, we were then taken to UNRRA quarters nearby where we had a proper bath and meal. After our meal, Hedda and I were then put back on the same train for the return trip to Stuttgart, Germany. However, we were both planning to get off the train when it reached Prague, Czechoslovakia.

What happened in Prague? Did you ever get to Warsaw?

Once in Prague, Hedda and I split up. I had a week's vacation saved up and wanted to visit the new Swedish children's hospital in Warsaw. The Swedish government had provided funds and built this hospital just after the war ended. I went off to the Polish consulate in Prague hoping to get a visa to visit Poland, and Hedda went off to search for missing relatives. Sadly, Hedda and I never saw each other again. Hedda was a very nice person, and I liked her.

Didn't Warsaw have numerous bombs strikes during the war. How did it look?

Pretty awful. After receiving my visa to enter Poland, I took the train from Prague to Warsaw. As we entered Warsaw, I could see it had been practically destroyed by the fighting between the Nazis and the Russians. The Jewish Ghetto in Warsaw had been totally flattened. It looked like a desert of stones.

But still, you were looking forward to seeing your Swedish friends who worked at a hospital for children with TB, located in Otwotsk, a suburb of Warsaw. Was that an enjoyable visit?

It was very nice to see many of my "old" nursing friends from Stockholm. I also met the sister of the famous Polish scientist, Madame Marie Curie. She was a teacher of the

Polish children who were at the Swedish hospital. Because of malnutrition and disease, many of these children had long hospital stays.

Did you see many Russian soldiers in Poland?

Yes. During my visit to Warsaw, I saw Russian troops and, again, Communist propaganda signs and slogans everywhere. One of the Polish nurses at the Swedish hospital asked one of my Swedish friends, "Why does your friend have an American uniform and carry a British passport?" My friend didn't know the answer so she asked me. I told her that my Swedish passport had expired, so I traveled with the British one. She cautioned me to be very careful. I, being naive about political intrigues, didn't think much of it. Basically, I felt very carefree.

Didn't you leave Warsaw and take a trip to Krakow in southern Poland?

Longing to see more of Poland, I followed up on a friend's suggestion to see Krakow because it had not been bombed during the war and was still quite beautiful. Because of the shortness of time, I booked a flight on an old transport plane from Warsaw to Krakow. When I landed in Krakow, I didn't know anyone there, but that didn't worry me as I love adventures.

This leg of your journey, however, became too adventurous. Didn't you have a serious encounter with the Soviet military? What happened?

After I had just gone to bed the first night at my hotel in

Krakow, I heard heavy banging on my hotel room door.

"What is it?" I asked in German, as I opened the door.

Three Russians carrying rifles on their backs and wearing military uniforms looked at me suspiciously and one of them asked in bad German, "We want to see your passport."

At that time the Russians were in charge of Poland. A shudder ran down my back for I knew that my Swedish passport had expired, and my British passport would be dangerous to show to Russian Communists.

I slowly walked over to my purse, pulled out my Swedish passport, and handed it over. I watched spellbound as the Russian soldier looked through the pages of my passport.

I was beginning to feel on tenderhooks as he slowly turned the pages.

I asked, "Is everything ok?"

I thought he smiled uneasily.

The Russian officer who laboriously flipped through the pages of my Swedish passport didn't notice the expired date. He just handed the passport back to me and said, "Excuse us. Don't be afraid."

They turned and walked out. My heart was pounding. I felt so relieved to be Swedish.

What did your friends say when you told them this story?

When I returned to Stuttgart, I told my friends at UNRRA about my passport ordeal in Krakow. One of them told me a scary thing: if I hadn't given the Russian my Swedish passport, but had handed over my British one, I would have been sent to a prison in Siberia. The Russians would have assumed I was a spy. Looking back, I remember feeling very happy I hadn't been shipped off to a Russian gulag.

Chapter 8

Weekend Adventures in Europe

While working at the United Nations in Stuttgart, you really led a charmed life? Didn't you meet the famous French singer, Maurice Chevalier? How did that happen?

I was not leading a charmed life actually—just leading the life of a working girl who had her weekends free.

But you took quite a few, interesting trips on the weekends when you had this job. Explain how you met Chevalier in Nice. Wasn't this in August of 1946?

Yes. I decided to take a short holiday from my job in Germany and travel to Nice. As Swedes, we had read that the Mediterranean coast of France was really lovely so I wanted to see it. Although I didn't know anyone in the French resort town of Nice, I soon met some Americans who were on vacation, as well. Ann Daniels, an American whom I met at the beach the day I arrived, made plans for us to attend a party one evening

Did Ann ask you a question while you were both sitting on the beach? How did you strike up a conversation since you were complete strangers relaxing in the sun?

Ann liked my two-piece bathing suit. It was considered

very daring in those days, but Swedes thought these suits were practical for tanning purposes. Ann had a wonderful personality and was quite talkative. She asked me, "Have you heard about this fabulous party in Nice called the La Nuit Blanche (The White Night) in which everyone has to dress in white?"

"No, but it sounds like fun," I replied.

"You have to wear white. Could you go?" she asked me.

"I don't have a white dress or skirt with me," I said, thinking that I had packed too lightly.

"But you could probably buy one or get one made quickly. Maurice Chevalier will be singing at this party so you don't want to miss it," Ann insisted.

"Ok" I said, as I hastily grabbed my beach blanket, shook it out, picked up my shoes and made plans to get back to my hotel immediately. I had to find a tailor to get a skirt made.

Did you actually get a white skirt made in two or three hours?

I bought a white sheet from my hotel manager and took it to a small sewing shop nearby. The ladies made a skirt in less than two hours. It cost less than $3.00. Fortunately, I had a white blouse with me, and with my custom made skirt and my nice tan, I looked fine.

What did the White Night Party look like? Was everything decorated in white? Were there hundreds of people in the streets?

The White Night Party was really special in 1946. After all, the famous French singer Maurice Chevalier provided the entertainment. Ann Daniels met me at the hotel, and we stood at the side of the main street in Nice and watched a big parade. The parade was splendid: People dressed in white were sitting in big carriages shaped like white swans. Everyone in the parade wore white and carried white flowers. Even the band members wore white uniforms.

Was Maurice Chevalier on a float in the parade?

No. He was at a private club nearby.

Wasn't he appearing in public for the very first time since the Second World War started? That must have been awe-inspiring?

I was very excited, along with everyone in this club. The audience stood up and cheered when he appeared on stage and began singing his classic, "Thank Heaven for Little Girls." He gave several encores—the crowd loved him.

So, how did you meet him?

On a lark, I decided to try to get Chevalier's autograph so I approached his assistant and asked, "Could I meet 'my favorite' French singer?"

Chevalier's assistant left me for a moment and returned and said, "Follow me." He led me to Chevalier's dressing room which greatly surprised me.

Chevalier welcomed me into his room and gave me an autographed picture of himself. We chatted for about 30 minutes. He told me he was planning to visit Stockholm soon and asked many questions about Sweden.

Did he ask you for a date?

No, I was wearing my engagement ring, and he saw it. I thought Chevalier was a very charming man; actually, I found him to be somewhat shy. Following that meeting, I returned to the club where everyone had started dancing. In those days women could easily exchange partners if someone did not suit them. Ann and I had a great time dancing with many different men dressed in white.

Did you end up leaving the club with a particular man?

No.

I recall that you saw Ann again at the historic military trials in Nuremberg, Germany. Describe this incredibly interesting weekend.

My holiday in Nice was followed three weeks later with an historic weekend trip to Nuremberg, Germany. On August 30, 1946, I hitchhiked to Nuremberg at the invitation of my now good American friend, Ann Daniels. Ann was working as one of the official UN stenographer typists at the war crimes trial of the 21 Nazi leaders held at the International Military Tribunal in Nuremberg.

You hitchhiked to Nuremberg alone? Wasn't that dangerous?

My British friend, Mildred, and I hitchhiked from Stuttgart to Nuremberg. Back in those days, we hitchhiked to save money in travel expenses. In the 1940's, it was safe for both men and women to hitch a ride. Since we were wearing our American Army uniforms, we didn't have a problem hitching a ride anywhere.

When you arrived in Nuremberg, was the town packed with people? Did you have a tough time finding your American friend Ann Daniels?

We were fortunate. There were hundreds of people milling around outside of the building where the trial took place! We saw Ann outside the court room, and she gave me a ticket to be seated in the press gallery. Since this was the conclusion of such an historical trial, there were plenty of people trying to get a pass to enter the courtroom. I entered the press area and during a break, I gave my ticket so Mildred so she could see the trail. Then I spotted Ann again, and she found an extra ticket for the visitor's section so I really spent the day at the trial.

Weren't the court proceedings in German?

Yes. And, I wore a headset so I could hear the court proceedings in English. I really didn't need it because I knew German, but I kept my headset on anyway so I wouldn't miss anything.

Were there many women in the room?

After I sat down in the press gallery and looked around, I noticed there were not many women attending the trial, maybe 10 of us. I felt extremely fortunate to be there.

Was it very emotional in the courtroom?

The room felt very tense, but no one cried or yelled. I heard several of the defendants say, "Nicht schuldig" which is "not guilty."

Did you see any famous German Nazi commanders?

I remember seeing Marshall Herman Göring, head of the German Air Force and one of the original members of Hitler's National Socialist Party. He had been very big and stout. But at the trial, his suit was hanging on him in folds. Rudolf Hess, who looked gaunt and bewildered, had a blanket around his waist.

Describe the scene at this historic trial?

There were eight judges in the court, plus 21 defendants and a battery of translators and staff. The 21 defendants sat in the room where you could clearly see them. This trial started on Nov. 21, 1945, before a panel of British, French, Russian and American judges, and it concluded on August 30, 1946.

Do you remember long speeches or anything noteworthy?

The longest statement of the day was given by Rudolf Hess who spoke for about 20 minutes. He looked lost and sort of rambled. Later I read and clipped a newspaper article that said all of the defendants had pleaded "not guilty."

Interestingly, one of the defendants, Hans Frank, changed his plea about six months later. I still have the newspaper report of April 18, 1947 in which he reportedly said, "I am guilty of the extermination of the Polish Jews. A thousand years will pass and the guilt of Germany will not be erased."

Do you have any mementos of this famous trial?

I still have a copy of the "Stars and Stripes" I picked up on

Sunday, September 1, 1946. Let me read it to you: "In its 217 days of session, the tribunal set many records unique in legal history. Court reporters took down 5,000,000 words uttered in court or roughly the equivalent of 25 novels the length of *Gone With the Wind.*

"Almost 22,000 visitors, from ambassadors to buck privates, witnessed the trials as spectators since it began on Nov. 20, 1945. The weary defendants intoned in 10,000 words their final excuses for executing Hitler's orders which brought death or misery to 25 million people."

Where did you go after the trial was over, back to Stuttgart?

After leaving Nuremberg, Mildred and I decided to hitch-hike to Austria. Unfortunately, Mildred did not have a visa to enter Austria. We hitched a ride on a truck near the border, and Mildred hid under some blankets in the back of the truck.

Our behavior was a bit risky! Our truck driver told the guard at the Austrian border that he had a sick GI in the back of the truck (Mildred), and we were waved on through.

So you were in Salzburg having a good time?

Once we reached Salzburg, we had a nice time because we were wearing our U.S. Army uniforms, and people had great respect for the American army. We had just missed the classical music festival in Salzburg by one day, but at least we saw the home of famous composer, Mozart. Salzburg was beautiful. Many people now generally know how it looks from that classic film, "The Sound of Music" which was filmed in several Salzburg locations.

Do you have any other interesting tales of traveling around Europe on the weekends?

About a month later, I went horse back riding in Germany with some friends. We could ride beautiful horses by giving the Germans a pack of American cigarettes—Luckies or Camels. On other weekend trips, we visited Heidelberg, saw the castle on top of a mountain in Hohenzollern, and climbed up to Hitler's Eagle Nest at Berchtesgaden. The view from Hitler's house was one of the best I've ever seen, surrounded by mountains with no other structures in the vicinity at that time.

Did you have any particular thoughts when looking at Hitler's home?

As I gazed at the beautiful view from Hitler's house, I asked myself why people had followed this crazy man. But looking at the history of the world, people often follow dictators singing their songs of hate. It's a universal mystery: why can't people embrace love, not hate?

I will never forget the contrasts between that courtroom in Nuremberg, what the defendants there had done, and the beautiful countryside in Germany and Austria.

Chapter 9

Vacation in Italy

What exactly did you do in your job for the United Nations?

I worked as a field secretary at the United Nation's Relief and Rehabilitation Administration in Stuttgart, Germany. During the last six months of this job, I distributed gifts to displaced persons and former Nazi prisoners of war (POWs) who now resided in Allied refugee camps.

It sounds like you were Ms. Santa Claus?

It was a terrific job; I gave people presents. With my own private chauffeur driving me around in an American army jeep, I visited camps in Germany where hundreds of displaced people still lived. When we arrived at a camp, I literally jumped out of the jeep and gave people games, sporting goods equipment and musical instruments. I also gave sewing and embroidery sets to the women.

Did you spend the night in various towns throughout Germany on these road trips?

My driver and I usually made these trips within an eight-hour period, a regular work day.

I imagine these displaced people were very happy to see you?

They were in high spirits when I arrived at a camp! I gave them nice gifts: guitars; accordions; and, badminton sets. I enjoyed this job, and knew I would miss it. So, I purposely waited until my work contract ended before taking a vacation and returning to Sweden.

Had you ever thought about settling down in England, your father's country?

No. Ultimately, I wanted to reside in Sweden. I felt lucky to have lived in a country that wasn't invaded or bombed during WW II. England, my father's birthplace, had not fared so well. It had been bombed repeatedly by the Germans.

Didn't you have a boy friend who lived in Germany at this time?

I met my fiancé, Stanislav Pilzak, a young engineering student from Czechoslovakia, in Germany. He was very attentive and romantic. We had taken wonderful weekend trips around Germany.

Although I was engaged to be married, I made plans to take a holiday to Switzerland and Italy without Stanislaw. He had to stay in Germany to finish his engineering studies at the university in Stuttgart.

Were you involved in a complete physical relationship with Stanislav?

I was deeply involved with him. We were engaged. At that

point in my life, I did not attend church and had no strong moral convictions about not having sex before marriage.

Describe your holiday in mid-March 1947?

As I mentioned, I made plans to visit Switzerland and Italy. It was a trip that perhaps in this day and age could be characterized as exciting as one in an American adventure film.

Because I still had my UN travel documents, I could book trains and hotels without any advance notice. In Italy, the American military had taken over most of the best Italian hotels, and American military and UN personnel could stay in rooms at unbelievably low prices. Looking through my old scrapbooks, I recently discovered a room receipt from my stay at a Naples hotel that only cost 15 cents per night!

You could board a train even at the last minute without a ticket because you wore an American Army uniform? How did that work?

Because I was employed by the UN, I was given American Army uniforms to wear to work every day. Since the Americans were operating special trains for American troops in Italy after the war, the conductors, who saw my uniform and UN travel documents, just allowed me to board without a ticket.

Here you are as happy as a lark visiting the best places in Europe for very little money, while most Europeans are struggling to put food on the table just after the war. Quite a contrast, wasn't it?

I was very lucky! At the age of 26, I had already seen many countries in Europe; I had a loving fiancé; and, I was in my American Army uniform getting ready to see the fantastic sights of Italy at a great price. After two weeks, I would return to Sweden and after two years, I would get married. Everything was turning out perfectly normal in my mind.

And, yet, I hesitated. Was Stanislav the right one to be my husband? Was there still more to do and see before finally settling down to be married? During the past several months, I had asked myself these questions several times a day, but I never had a definitive answer.

Were you praying for some answers to your questions or were you too busy living an exciting life? What did love mean to you?

Love meant having good feelings about someone. I was not very religious at that point. It never occurred to me to pray to God about anything that bothered me. And, I was having an exciting and interesting life. I assumed the good times would continue.

Let's return to your vacation trip to Switzerland and Italy. What did you do in Switzerland?

I stayed with a Swiss couple, who I had worked with at the UN in Stuttgart. They showed me Geneva and then helped me arrange a fabulous trip throughout Switzerland. I skied in St. Moritz and took a railway up to Die Jungfrau, about 4,000 meters above sea level. At the highest point, I left the train and skied back down to a hotel at the bottom of Die Jungfrau. I saw all the most beautiful places in Switzerland, and it wasn't too expensive. While working in Germany, I had saved money for this trip to Italy and Switzerland, as I knew I was moving back to Sweden, and it would be a long time before I could take such trips again.

Next, you boarded a train to Milan, Italy. However, you had quite a shock when your train pulled into Milan. What happened?

As I sat on the train headed for Milan, I felt great. I sat in the first-class dining car of the train, smoking a cigarette and drinking a cup of coffee. For 30 minutes, I consciously savored the comfort and elegance of it all.

Then, the train stopped, and I walked out of the train station in Milan thinking about which places I should visit. My reverie was interrupted by the noise of people rioting.

I was truly shocked! The Italians there were rioting in the streets in what is now known as a "historic, anti-American riot."

I've read that in the early stages of the Second World War, the Italian leader, Mussolini, had been allied with Hitler, but he was overthrown on July 24, 1943. His replacement was Marshal Cavallero, who had begun secret armistice talks with the Allies. Hitler, suspecting that the Italians wanted out of the war, had sent German reinforcements into northern Italy to safeguard his connections to Italy. His propaganda efforts in the press had resulted in an intense dislike for the Allies in northern Italy. Did you know that at the time?

No. But I later learned the Italians were protesting the terms of a peace treaty recently signed by Allied leaders that was not advantageous to Italy. I saw people in Milan throwing stones at Allied vehicles and ripping down signs. I actually saw Italians pull down an American flag that had flown on top of one of the buildings. Basically, I was surrounded by desperate people who had lost the war and were angry at the Americans for their involvement in this conflict.

Here you are in the middle of a riot, and you don't know a soul. What did you do next?

Luckily, a sympathetic Italian man, who appeared worried about my safety, pushed me aggressively into a shop where I was safe from potential harm. He yelled, "Go to your hotel at once and stay there." I immediately obeyed him and ran out the back door to my hotel that was about two blocks away.

Once you reached your hotel, did you stay there for the night?

Yes. But, I couldn't wait to get out of Milan; so the next day, I took a taxi from my hotel to the train station with plans to leave on the next available train. I was hoping to catch a train to Florence, but any train departing Milan would suffice. Unfortunately, it had started snowing in Milan.

After I jumped out of the taxi and rushed up to the ticket counter at central station, I was told "finito." All trains had stopped running for the day. I stood at the station, holding my suitcase and watching this tremendous snow storm. For once in my life, I felt helpless. Fortunately, a GI who noticed my American Army uniform appeared as my guardian angel.

"Can I help you?" he asked, looking at my nervous face and carefully scrutinizing my American Army uniform. I told him all the departing trains had been cancelled because of the snow, and I didn't know what to do.

"Well, I can take you to a nice hotel in Milan, and perhaps you can leave tomorrow," he said, as he grabbed my suitcase. We started walking to his army jeep outside of the station. Moreover, he took me to one of the best hotels in Milan, which the Americans had taken over. Again, it only cost me 15 cents to spend the night there!

What happened next?

The following day, I took a taxi to Milan's central station and boarded a train to Florence. I was disappointed to learn that many of the famous paintings were unavailable and were stored in cellars because of the war.

Then, you left Florence for Rome. I recall you met Pope Pius XII in Rome. How did you pull that off?

I traveled by train to Rome and, by chance, met a group of Americans who had scheduled an audience with Pope Pius XII. They invited me to join them.

How many of you were in the group?

I remember there were about 12 of us standing in a room in the Vatican. When Pope Pius XII came into the room, all the Americans fell to their knees. I, being Swedish and Protestant, just stood there smiling. All the Catholics in the group kissed his ring. I shook his hand. After Pope Pius XII shook my hand, he initiated a conversation with me. Frankly, I was surprised. In a serious tone, he asked me where I was from and what work did I do. We had a small conversation.

What did Pope Pius XII look like?

He was tall and thin and had piercing dark brown eyes behind gold-rimmed glasses.

What did you talk about with the Pope?

We talked about Sweden. And, he asked me about my work at the UN. After our conversation, the Pope took a few steps back, and looked at me rather reflectively. In retrospect, I think he was saying a quick prayer on my behalf. Then, he turned to a man standing behind him who held a silver tray covered with medals. He picked one up and gave it to me—a medal engraved with his picture.

How did that encounter affect you? Did you think more seriously about God and religion?

Yes. I did become more interested in going to church. Now, that I am a Catholic, I remember that meeting with great joy. And, I still have that medal.

Wasn't Pope Pius XII (1876-1958) considered to be a Pope who didn't help the Jews much during World War II?

I think the recent charges are ungrounded. I believe he did his best to help the Jews during the war, but he did it secretly. Also, after the war, Jewish leaders such as Golda Meir praised him for all that he had done to help the Jewish people.

So you truly believe he was a very good Pope?

This Pope made a great impression on me when we met. He had very special eyes that were very somber, and he radiated holiness. I read recently that he is still very much loved and respected by many people, including Pope John Paul II.

Where did you go after you visited Rome?

After meeting the Pope, I decided to travel to Naples and, after that, to Sorrento with an American woman, Linda Smith, whom I had met in Rome. We stayed at "The Victoria," a five star hotel with a great view of the sea and Mount Vesuvius. The next day, we decided to walk to the top of Mount Vesuvius, because as Linda put it, we would have a "fabulous view."

Luckily, we were joined by six American servicemen who had seen us in Sorrento the night before. They joined us on our adventurous walk to the top of Mount Vesuvius.

When we started walking up the mountain, I was so glad I wore my heavy walking shoes—a good purchase made in Switzerland. Linda, on the other hand, wore crocodile leather, high heeled shoes, and, needless to say, she had a tough time walking almost two hours up this hot mountain.

What did you do when you got to the top of the mountain? Take pictures?

When we reached the top, we all wanted a cigarette, but we had forgotten our lighters and matches. Linda, who was very resourceful, just bent down, and with her foot scraped away the top level of soil and lit her cigarette on the hot ashes under the soil. We smiled and followed her example. After admiring the view and enjoying our cigarette break, I decided to venture down into the volcano's crater where actual wisps of smoke drifted up from different places.

"Does anyone want to go with me down into the crater?" I asked. Three of the men laughed and one said, "Let's go!"

Did you need a man's help to descend into this volcano?

Not really. We didn't go that far into the crater, but I wanted to take a picture and thought that by going down into the crater, I would snap a prize-winning shot. We walked down a few yards into the crater. I took a couple of pictures between coughing fits. It was hot and smoky! Luckily, the volcano wasn't active. We later learned that there had been an outburst of ashes and heavy smoke one year earlier!

You were lucky the volcano wasn't active! Where did you go next?

Walking down from the top of Mount Vesuvius was tiring and took about 90 minutes, but we still had the energy to visit Pompeii, the ancient Italian city which had been buried in ash from an eruption of the nearby volcano, Mount Vesuvius.

Following our tour of Pompeii, I said good-bye to Linda, my American friend and my traveling companions and bought myself a ticket on a small boat that made daily excursions to the Isle of Capri. After arriving at this island, I decided to see the Blue Grotto, a special body of water on the coast of Capri.

What is the Blue Grotto?

The Blue Grotto is actually a body of water that exists in an underwater tunnel near Anacapri. As the sunlight passes through the underwater cavity, it shines through the seawater and creates a blue reflection that illuminates the cavern.

One enters the cave by a small row boat through a low and narrow opening. Then you travel to the sides of the cave which open to form an oval measuring roughly a 100 meters from one end to the other. The light coming through the opening of the cave creates a wonderful luminosity.

I recall you told me once that an Italian boat driver in Capri almost sexually attacked you on this trip?

Not really. When I saw this friendly-looking Italian man, about 40, who knew a tiny bit of English, I asked him to take me to the Blue Grotto in his row boat.

I was a bit nervous because he didn't know very much English, and I couldn't speak Italian. He smiled and rowed me into this dark cave. I had been in this boat for about 45 minutes, and it was pitch black inside the cave. The boat owner just kept speaking Italian in a low, sexy-sounding voice. I became worried.

Were you contemplating jumping overboard?

Not really. Fortunately, I heard some people speaking English in row boats nearby, so I yelled, "Help! Help! Please take me to your boat."

There were about six little row boats nearby filled with men dressed in military uniforms. They rowed their boats over to me.

"Can we help you?" one of the servicemen asked.

"Yes," I replied. "I want to get out of this boat and into yours."

"Of course," one of the men said, and helped me into his boat as the other men sat there smiling. He rowed us out of the cave and over to a military ship—a huge American battleship. I was in my American Army uniform, a real blessing in this situation.

Now you are on a U.S. battleship in the Mediterranean Sea, and the only woman on a ship with thousands of men. How did that feel?

I had a great time! Marvin A. Oreck, Lt. Commander on this U.S. battleship in the Mediterranean, near Capri, was my escort for the evening. Although I can't remember the name of the battleship now, I do remember seeing one of the latest American movies on board, as well as having dinner in a lovely dining room near the officers' quarters. After we docked, Lt. Commander Oreck took me to a hotel in Naples where his staff helped me get on one of the Italian tour boats to Sorrento. From Sorrento, I took another boat to Capri where I booked a hotel room, left my things, and started walking around. (There weren't many tourists in Southern Italy back then—too close to the end of the war.)

Why did you want to visit Capri?

I wanted to see San Michele, a famous house on Capri. I had read about this villa in a book, *The Story of San Michele,* by Axel Munthe, a Swedish physician. Many Swedes had been fascinated by this memoir which had received major press attention world-wide. San Michele is a huge villa that had been purchased and remodeled by Dr. Munthe, who had spent most of his life practicing medicine in such places as Paris and Rome. Also, he was Swedish Queen Victoria's personal physician and very good friend.

When was *The Story of San Michele* published, and was it

still selling well in 1947?

Yes. It was first published in 1929. And, it's been printed in some 45 languages and gone through at least 30 editions. It's still selling briskly, even in 2002.

Were you hoping to meet Dr. Munthe, the author of this best-selling memoir?

No. I knew he was in Sweden, but I wanted to see his house. Now, I know why Dr. Munthe left Capri: the Italian entry into the war forced him to consider a safer place to live. Also, he had asthma and a bad heart.

Were you very impressed with his villa on Capri?

It was magnificent. Inside were marble statutes and fragments of Greek and Roman carvings, as well as marble rooms filled with treasures dug from many ancient ruins. Dr. Munthe, an amateur archeologist, had collected unusual things from Italy and the Middle East.

I have read that this home has an incredible view. Does it?

I think San Michele has one of the best views in the world.

Who was in charge of his villa while Dr. Munthe was in Sweden?

His Italian housekeeper. When I knocked on the door of this villa, I was greeted by Erminia Lucca, the housekeeper. He had put her in charge when he left for Stockholm.

How did you and Erminia strike up a conversation? Did she speak English?

She spoke a little English. Erminia asked me to sign the address book in the hall because she kept a record of all visitors to San Michele. When I wrote down my name and my future address in Stockholm, she looked at me rather strangely.

Why?

Erminia left me alone for a minute and then returned with a letter. I understood her to be asking me, "Could you deliver this letter yourself to Axel Munthe, who now lives at the castle in Stockholm?"

I said, "I'll try," as I tucked the letter into my purse.

Didn't Dr. Munthe's housekeeper then phone Baroness Uexkull, a Swede, who asked to speak to you while you were still walking through the house? Why?

The Baroness, who was staying at the other villa on Axel Munthe's property, Torre di Materita, was intrigued that a Swede, dressed in an American Army uniform, was touring the property. She invited me to lunch.

Describe that luncheon.

Joining us at this luncheon was Dr. Brilliot, the editor of Stockholm's morning daily newspaper *Stockholms Tidningen* at the time, and his daughter. It was just a coincidence that they just happened to be visiting Capri at the same time I was.

During the lunch, the Baroness and Dr. Brilliot discussed the fact that Dr. Munthe never really had spent much time at his lovely villa. He was always traveling to countries throughout Europe.

You have read *The Story of San Michele.* Why do you think Axel Munthe's book became so popular?

Axel Munthe was very intelligent and provocative. He left Sweden when he was 17 and became the youngest medical student in France up until that time. Later, he practiced medicine in Paris and Rome and was considered one of the best physicians on the continent. Also, he helped the poor and suffering. He had treated Italians fighting a cholera epidemic in the 1890's; he assisted victims of the Messina, Italy earthquake in 1908; and he provided medical care to soldiers on the front lines in World War I from 1914 to 1918.

How did he discover the island of Capri?

I heard it was Queen Victoria of Sweden who had introduced Dr. Munthe to Capri.

When did Dr. Munthe become Queen Victoria's personal physician?

When he returned to Stockholm for a brief period in 1890, at the age of 33, he became her personal physician.

Is it true that he had very rich patients and many gave him expensive gifts when he successfully treated their illnesses?

Yes. He had a stained-glass window given to him by the great actress Eleanora Duse, as well as many other things given to him by the rich and famous around the world.

Chapter 10

Walks with Axel Munthe

When did you contact Dr. Munthe?

After I returned to Stockholm from Italy, I called the palace and asked to speak to Dr. Munthe. Unfortunately, he was not listed in the palace telephone directory.

Then, what?

I called my good friend, Countess Thott. She was a physical therapist, who was then giving treatments to Prince Bertil, one of the king's nephews who also lived at the palace in Stockholm. She gave me Dr. Munthe's home phone number. When I reached Dr. Munthe, I began chatting about his lovely home in Capri and told him I had a letter for him.

"Just post the letter," he said gruffly.

Did you feel discouraged?

I changed tactics.

I said, "I have a message for you from Baroness Uexkull." Instantly, his manner and voice changed. He said in a soft voice, "Please come to the palace at six o'clock tomorrow, and my valet will meet you and escort you to my apartment."

How did you get to the castle?

I took the bus. My apartment, located in Gardet, was not too far from the castle. Vittorio Masemino, Dr. Munthe's valet, met me at the entrance and escorted me to his apartment. Vittorio was the brother of Erminia Lucca, the housekeeper at San Michele. She was the one who had given me the letter to Axel Munthe.

Was Dr. Munthe's apartment fantastic?

No, not at all. It was just the opposite from what I had expected—very somber and dark. The apartment was strange in appearance because the Swedish royal family had recently rebuilt the palace, and they had converted two stories out of one. Some might call the results an architectural mistake. Dr. Munthe's apartment had windows that reached down to the floor and that looked strange. The furniture was dull. And, overall, the apartment was chilly.

Was Dr. Munthe, at 90, a good conversationalist? Did he have short-term memory loss?

He was very warm and friendly, and his memory was excellent. We spoke together for about 90 minutes, and he asked me about Capri, the Blue Grotto, the birds, and the gardens.

I told him about some of my experiences at the United Nations and about my family. He was impressed that my brother, an ornithologist, had written several books on that topic.

When did he decide he wanted to see you again?

When I was putting on my coat to leave, Dr. Munthe

asked, "Would you be my walking companion if I called you once in a while?"

I replied, "I'd be happy to walk with you, but it has to be scheduled after my work day."

About a week later, he called me. We set a date to meet for a walk. I was working at Scandinavian Airlines (SAS) in the personnel department in charge of foreign pilots.

For the next year and a half, Dr. Munthe called me at my SAS office. My colleagues would joke about his calls, mimicking his voice, which was very low and loud. Frankly, I was very flattered that Dr. Munthe, himself, called me.

Where did you walk in Stockholm? Did people know who he was? Did you feel very important?

We usually walked in Gamla Stan, the older section of Stockholm. The second time we met, Dr. Munthe wore a dark cape and carried a walking stick.

He asked me if I would like a walking stick, as well.

I said yes, so he handed me a beautiful stick, stating "This belonged to Queen Victoria."

I felt very relaxed with Dr. Munthe. Although I knew how famous he was, I really didn't think about it when we took our walks.

Did people come up to Dr. Munthe and start talking about his book?

I remember one evening we ran into Vera. Vera was well known for saving the old section of Stockholm from modernization. She was frequently in the newspapers. Upon meeting us, she called him "Tiberius" and practically flirted with him.

How did she flirt with him? Did she ask him for a date?

In a way, yes. She asked if she could go to Capri with him.

However, her offer didn't appeal to Dr. Munthe. He turned away from her and whispered to me, "Here one meets someone he would like to take to Capri, but she is engaged (meaning me). I would never take her (Vera) to Capri because she would just use it to get her name in the newspapers."

I take it Axel Munthe didn't like aggressive women?

Not at all. He had had a bitter marriage to a wealthy British woman, Hilda, and they had been separated a long time.

Did he talk about Hilda and his sons?

He never said a word about her or his two sons to me, but he was quite a conversationalist during our walks.

Did he tell you some interesting stories about his life?

He told me that he was one of the amateur archeologists who had assisted in opening King Tutankhamen's tomb in Egypt!

Do you mean the famous King Tut? What's the story?

King Tutankhamen (King Tut) was the youngest pharaoh of ancient Egypt, just 9, when he took the throne and 18 when he died, 3200 years ago. British archaeologist Howard Carter led a group of scientists and friends, including Axel

Munthe, to the tomb of King Tut and opened it on November 26, 1922.

The fabulous riches in the tomb of King Tut have been documented in many books and films and exhibitions. Five thousand objects, including lots of gold, were buried with King Tut to keep him happy in his afterlife. Did he tell you how he escaped the "curse of the pharaoh?"

He was amazed he had escaped the "curse of the pharaoh." Lord Carnarvon, the first to enter King Tut's tomb, died a terrible death six months later. Also, American archeologists Arthur Mace and George Jay Gould both died within 24 hours of entering the tomb.

Why did he think he had escaped from that tomb without a serious illness?

Dr. Munthe told me it was extraordinary that he did not die quickly after that expedition. All his friends died mysterious deaths soon after they opened that tomb.

"Why do you think they died?" I asked him.

"It's a great mystery!" he whispered.

He asked me if I had seen the snake ring he took from King Tut's tomb? When I said no, he showed me a ring on his ring finger made of gold in the shape of a snake with real emeralds as snake eyes.

"When I die," he stated dramatically, "they will probably dig up my grave and open my casket just to get this ring!"

I just laughed, and said, "You may be right."

Didn't he always wear dark glasses when he was outside?

He usually wore dark glasses, and once said, "I've always been afraid of losing my sight."

"Is that why you wear dark glasses?" I asked him.

"I wear dark glasses," he said, "because the sun's brightness is too much of a strain for my eyes." He told me his eyes had been damaged by a burst of light that appeared when King Tut's tomb was opened. And, he said, the sunlight at his villa in Capri had also hurt his eyesight.

Although Dr. Munthe wore dark glasses and used a walking stick, you recently told me you thought his eyesight was surprisingly good. Why?

Once he said, "You shouldn't wear lipstick because your lips are very pleasant without it."

"You must have good eyes to have noticed that I was wearing lipstick!" I replied.

Didn't Dr. Munthe miss his beautiful villa in Italy?

Very much. During our walks, Dr. Munthe often told me how much he missed his villa on Capri and seeing the thousands of birds there. In fact, he told me how he had saved the birds near his villa on Capri. The story is similar to one he wrote in his book, *The Story of San Michele.*

What happened?

Every year, huge flocks of birds migrated to Capri. This phenomenon was one of the reasons Axel Munthe loved Capri so much.

As the story goes, there was a man, an ex-butcher, who owned hill property on the mountain of Barbarosssa, one of the areas where the birds congregated. He would net the birds and kill them. Sometimes he netted more than 1,000 birds a day, including larks, quails, nightingales, thrushes and swallows, especially during a particular season.

Dr. Munthe appealed to the local authorities, to the Italian local and national governments to stop this man from killing the birds. He tried shooting his gun to scare the birds off or by using barking dogs. He offered huge sums of money to buy this man out. He even tried to maim the ex-butcher in a fight. Nothing worked.

Was he ever successful in stopping the man who was shooting all those birds?

His success was something of a miracle. The man who killed all these birds suddenly became very ill, and no one was able to diagnose his illness. Dr. Munthe offered to treat him but only on the grounds that if he were healed, he would stop killing birds. The man agreed and sure enough Dr. Munthe successfully diagnosed and treated the man's pleurisy.

Capri is now a bird sanctuary.

I've read he was a real animal lover. He would be right at home in today's world, don't you think?

Absolutely. He once said to me, "The air in the palace doesn't suit me. The king is talking too much about hunting."

Did Dr. Munthe talk about his books and writing career with you?

One day, he called me at home and asked me to go to the Nobel Library, a famous institution in Stockholm, and borrow a book.

The book, *Red Cross and Iron Cross*, was another that Dr. Munthe had written. He said he had recently received a telegram from a famous Hollywood director who wanted to make a movie based on his experiences as a doctor in France during WWI.

In this book, Dr. Munthe was very critical of the Germans during WW I. But, because they had lost that war and the Second World War, he felt sorry for them. He told me, "One does not strike a country that is already down." He told me he bought every copy of his book he could find and burned them except the one left on the shelves of the Nobel Library. I later learned there were other copies of this book in England and around Sweden.

What was your reaction to his request?

I was very touched and said to him, "You must be very honored that someone in Hollywood would like to make a movie about your book."

"Not really," he replied. "I would like to know what you think."

I promptly did as he requested and read the book. I thought it was very interesting and told him it would make a great movie. During the war, I worked with the Swedish Red Cross and visited a German concentration camp. As I had seen the atrocities committed by the Nazis first-hand, I said to him: "You should let them make a film so these kinds of things won't happen again."

Did he take your advice?

Dr. Munthe seemed undecided on what to do when I left

him that day.

The next day, he told me, "I will not let Hollywood have the rights to make this film. But, if I did let them make the film, I would give my royalties to the German children."

During one of your walks together, Dr. Munthe asked you to be his private nurse. Why did you turn him down?

He wanted me to be his private secretary and nurse. King Gustav of Sweden had given permission for me to live and work at the palace. I was very flattered that Dr. Munthe wanted me to work for him, but I knew I had to check with my fiancé before accepting such an offer.

When I telephoned my fiancé Stanislaw in Germany and asked him what he thought about this offer, he was strongly opposed to the idea. We discussed it for a while, but I could sense that Stanislaw felt threatened by this opportunity for me to live and work in the palace. It would have been a very glamorous setting.

So I told Dr. Munthe I couldn't accept his offer.

What was his reaction? I imagine he was surprised?

He couldn't believe it. He said loudly: "They are standing in a queue at the British Embassy to be my secretary, and they are standing in a queue at the Red Cross to be my nurse. How can you turn me down?"

Yes. How could you?

It wasn't easy. He wanted me to be his secretary because he was writing three books at the same time.

What were the books about?

One was titled, *The Tragedy of Getting Old.* The second book was to be called, *Death and the Doctor*, and the third book was about Queen Victoria. King Gustav had given Dr. Munthe permission to write a biography of the king's deceased wife.

Did he offer to take you to San Michele in Capri?

Yes. He told me if I was his nurse, he would take me to St. Michele, and give me an Italian Madonna or a Greek Goddess statue, whichever I preferred. When I said I couldn't, he confessed, "I'm not used to begging a woman to be with me."

I'm sure Dr. Munthe was not used to being turned down by any woman.

Looking back, I think he probably enjoyed my company more because I didn't fawn over him. I treated him as if he was just an ordinary person, not a celebrity, and I think he secretly liked that.

Can you recall any other interesting sessions with Dr. Munthe?

One evening, when Dr. Munthe and I walked around Gamla Stan, I noticed that all the drunken men were waving and smiling at us.

When I looked at Dr. Munthe with a quizzical look, he said, "I have given all the drunks on the streets free beer every Christmas since I've lived at the palace."

Was he ever seriously ill when you were with him?

Once, one cold winter day when I visited him, I thought he looked very tired. I asked him, "How are you feeling today?"

He replied,"I've been sitting up most of the night with my asthma. Last night I saw Death sitting in this chair," and he held up his walking stick and pointed to a chair next to the bed.

He could be very dramatic.

Do you think Axel Munthe was a spiritual seeker?

He really admired the Little Sisters of the Poor, and I think he believed God existed.

One of my favorite passages from his book, *The Story of San Michele* is the one in which he writes: "All that is really beautiful is not put up for sale but is offered as a gift: The sunrise, the sunset, forest, fields, the glorious sea, birds singing for us, and wild flowers blooming along the road."

Did you see him after he had hired a full-time nurse?

No. Unfortunately, I never saw him again. I had to travel to England to visit my father and when I returned two weeks later, Dr. Munthe had hired a nurse. He died two years later. Actually, my mother attended his funeral which she said was truly beautiful and very well attended. I was abroad when he passed away and unfortunately couldn't attend the service. Dr. Munthe once spoke with my mother on the phone and told her that she had a very sweet voice. She was a very big fan of his, too.

Chapter 11

SAS Ground Hostess

What did you do after you left your job with the UN?

After I returned to Sweden in the summer of 1947, I accepted a position with Scandinavian Airlines Systems (SAS) at Stockholm International Airport in the nearby suburb of Bromma. My job was to assist foreign pilots in Stockholm; however, they usually only needed to find short term rental apartments. It was rather uninteresting work.

I imagine you were quite bored considering your exciting adventures at the UN. Did you look for a new position within the SAS organization?

Yes. To my good fortune, six months after I started working for SAS, the chief ground hostess left to marry an American pilot, and I got her job.

Wasn't this job similar to that of an airline hostess, pushing a trolley cart around and serving soft drinks to passengers?

Very similar. But, in this case, passengers were served in the airport lounge before boarding their planes. I also supervised two assistants.

Did you do anything more for the Swedish Red Cross after you started working for SAS?

I still had my connections with the Swedish Red Cross. After several months with SAS, I received a call from Count Folke Bernadotte's office. They asked me to assist the Spanish delegation attending the International Red Cross Conference in Stockholm in the fall of 1947. I happily agreed to do so. I had been studying Spanish once a week after work, so I was more than happy to spend a long weekend speaking with national Spanish speakers.

Sadly, that was the last time I saw Folke Bernadotte alive. Immediately after this meeting, he returned to Jerusalem where he was killed by extremists. (See earlier discussion in chapter on "White Buses in Germany.")

Didn't you meet the famous Swedish movie star, Ingrid Bergman, as a SAS ground hostess?

Yes. I met Sweden's famous actress at Stockholm's International Airport in Bromma. She and her daughter Pia, who was about six-years-old, and her first husband, Dr. Aron Petter Lindström, arrived at the airport in Bromma one Saturday in early 1948. Because the Swedish press knew Ingrid Bergman was leaving Sweden for the United States, there were many photographers and people milling about. All were hoping to have a chance to meet her and take her picture.

What did you do to protect her from the crowd?

To avoid the gathering crowds hoping to see her, we modified our usual procedures. I accompanied Ingrid Bergman, and her family, along with a government customs official to a plane out on the runway. On the plane, we stamped the passports, which freed one of the world's most famous actresses from being overwhelmed by fans.

What was Ingrid Bergman like?

She was charming and very beautiful. As it took some time to get the passports inspected and stamped, we had about a 15-minute conversation on board the plane.

What did you discuss with her?

I told her that she had made it possible for me to get into Poland when I was working for the United Nations. I described my trip to Poland to repatriate 600 Poles (former inmates and POWs) from Germany back to Poland. I told her that I couldn't enter Poland because I didn't have a visa to enter the country. (I explained that I only had one week's vacation and had to get a visa quickly in order to see my Swedish friends who were working at a new Swedish children's hospital outside of Warsaw.)

Getting this visa took a little acting on your part, if I remember correctly?

Not acting, persistence! I had taken the train to Czechoslovakia from the Polish border. Now, I was in Prague and had to see the Polish Consulate there in order to get a visa to enter Poland. You must remember that the Soviet Union had taken over Poland by this time and permission to travel to Soviet bloc countries was difficult to obtain.

Were you wearing your American uniform?

I always wore it. Someone at the Polish Consulate told me I had to wait three weeks for a visa to enter Poland. Fortunately, the Polish Consul in Prague became very interested in my case because I was Swedish. He told me he just loved "that Swedish movie star Ingrid Bergman," and as he was going to Poland the next day, he would personally make sure I had a visa within two days. He delivered on his promise—I had my visa in record time.

How did Ingrid Bergman react to your story?

She laughed. She was very charming. I complimented her on her work in such films as *"Casablanca"* with Humphrey Bogart; *"Notorious"* with Cary Grant; and *"Gas Light"* with Charles Boyer. Her husband, Dr. Lindström, spoke to me in a friendly manner, too. I actually knew him from my nursing days at St. Erik's Hospital in Stockholm.

You knew Ingrid Bergman's husband. How well?

Dr. Lindström had originally trained to be a dentist in Sweden. However, when World War II began, Sweden needed more doctors, so they recruited Swedish dentists. To become a doctor, a dentist could take an intensive medical training course, although for a much shorter time period than regular medical studies. Dr. Lindström signed up to become a medical doctor. He and I were on the same floor of St. Erik's Hospital in Stockholm—where I was training to be a war nurse.

Did Dr. Lindström chat with you frequently when you were training to be a nurse then?

Dr. Lindström constantly asked me questions about nursing procedures to the extent that the head nurse told me not to answer his questions but to send him to her instead. Now years later, it occurred to me as we were chatting that he had become a famous brain surgeon in the United States.

Did you meet other American movie stars traveling by plane to and from Sweden?

No, but my time with SAS from 1947 to 1948 was an adventure-filled experience.

Did you meet other Swedish celebrities who were traveling to and from Sweden?

Yes. I had dinner and breakfast with Sweden's famous opera singer, Jussi Björling and his wife. Before meeting Ingrid Bergman, I had to relocate to Copenhagen, Denmark for three months because the SAS ground personnel went on strike in Sweden. All SAS passengers with tickets to the USA were detoured through Copenhagen via train to Malmö, and then they took the ferry to Copenhagen. As chief ground hostess, I accompanied SAS passengers on the train from Stockholm to the ferry depot in Copenhagen and made sure they were driven to their hotel. The next day, I would get them on a bus to the airport.

Describe that experience of dining with one of the world's greatest tenors.

Because of the strike in Stockholm, I was asked to accompany the SAS passengers, who included Jussi Björling and his wife, to Copenhagen. When I met the passengers in the various cars of the train, Jussi and his wife asked me to join them in the dining car. In fact, he pulled out a carnation from a huge bouquet of flowers that he was holding, and gave it to me.

Do you remember what you ate?

We all had beer and sausages.

Did Jussi and his wife tell any interesting stories about their travels?

I had a rather funny experience with Sweden's greatest opera singer. He started telling me a story, and I was just half-listening. I wasn't trying to be rude, but I had to keep my eyes on all the SAS passengers on the ferry from Malmö to Copenhagen; I was very preoccupied.

Anyway, as Jussi was talking, he started laughing his head off. When I asked him why he was laughing, he said, "I told you the waves in the channel between Sweden and Denmark were so rough that several train cars fell into the sea."

"Really," I replied.

He thought it was so funny that I believed him, although I had not really listened to what he had said.

He was supposed to be one of the world's greatest tenors. Did you ever see him in concert?

Yes. I saw both he and his wife in "*La Boheme*" by

Puccini. His wife was singing opposite him for a performance in Stockholm. They were fabulous! The performance was in honor of the delegates who were attending an international Red Cross conference. Interestingly, it was probably the last performance Count Folke Bernadotte saw, as well, because he left for Palestine a couple of days later and was killed. I was a volunteer assisting the Spanish delegation at this conference.

Did you go backstage to see Jussi Björling.

Unfortunately, I did not. Looking back, I thought he was a very pleasant and nice man.

I imagine air travel was a lot more difficult in the 1940s?

Back then, planes only left the ground when the weather cooperated. As it happened, in the fall of 1947, Copenhagen experienced many rainy and foggy days. Consequently, many flights were delayed. As a result, I became friendly with some of the passengers because I was in charge of their schedules in Denmark while they were waiting to depart for the United States.

So poor weather meant fine dining?

Yes. I ate at Copenhagen's choice restaurants and saw great theatrical productions with first class passengers.

Did you ever become romantically involved with any of the passengers?

I didn't become romantically involved with anyone, but some of the passengers invited me to America. Two of them invited me to be guests in their homes in the United States.

Did you accept their invitations? Did you spend some time in the United States?

I gladly accepted their invitations. One passenger, Richard Söderberg, of Swedish descent, was a professor at Massachusetts Institute of Technology in Boston. He invited me to his home outside Boston. I accepted his invitation and stayed with his wife, daughter and two sons, who were in their early twenties. They showed me the sights of Boston, and I had a wonderful time.

Didn't you take flying lessons with one of the passengers?

Another passenger, Tor Solberg, also invited me to America. Tor Solberg owned an airfield in New Jersey and trained pilots. He was the first Norwegian to cross the Atlantic Ocean by plane from the United States to Norway. While I was visiting him in New Jersey, one of my Swedish male friends was training to be a pilot at his airfield. My friend, the new pilot, and I went up in a Piper Cub and flew over New York City, the first time my Swedish friend had ever piloted a plane with a passenger.

Is this the time you actually flew a plane near the Statue of Liberty?

We had a great time flying around Manhattan and the Statue of Liberty. And, I helped fly the plane as the assistant pilot. I actually was flying the plane when we headed back to New Jersey. Fortunately, we didn't crash, and landed safely back at the airfield in New Jersey.

Did you have other adventures that you can remember?

During a flight back to Copenhagen from New York on an SAS plane, my boss asked me if I would be the "Lucia" and take my assistants along as helpers.

What does it mean to be a Lucia?

St. Lucia Day is a traditional Swedish holiday that is celebrated on December 13. A young girl, with candles blazing on her head, wears a long white robe and sings a melodic tune about an Italian saint, St. Lucia of Syracuse.

Traditionally, Lucia mornings are celebrated in practically every Swedish home, office and school. The Lucia is dressed in a white gown and wears a crown of candles in her hair. She brings a tray of coffee and saffron rolls and ginger cookies to those awaiting her. Lucia is generally accompanied by her attendants, also dressed in white. The girls wear glitter in their hair, and boys wear tall paper cones with stars on them. All sing melodic Lucia carols in celebration of this wonderful tradition.

Do the Danes celebrate St. Lucia Day?

No, Sweden is the only Scandinavian country that celebrates St. Lucia Day.

You became Lucia one morning for SAS passengers from Stockholm who had been re-routed through Copenhagen. How did that work?

On Dec. 13, 1947, my attendants and I—all dressed in white robes, started knocking on doors of the SAS passengers at the Österport Hotel in Copenhagen. We started knocking on these hotel doors at seven o'clock in the morning.

At first, people were astonished to see us and then thrilled when we started singing and serving them fresh saffron buns and coffee. Many joked that they thought they had died and gone to heaven because we looked like angels in our costumes. I thoroughly enjoyed it as I love to sing, although I sing for fun only. Our picture even appeared on the front page of the Danish evening paper that day! In all, it was a great public relations success for SAS.

How long did your job last with SAS?

My job as ground hostess didn't last more than a year because I fell in love and wanted to marry Stefan Petersen, a station manager for a major airline in Stockholm.* Back then, if you married, you lost your job as a stewardess or ground hostess. In those days, the major airlines only employed single women.

During my last week at SAS, I received a letter from Mr. Grant, the SAS chief of ground personnel worldwide. He wrote, "Karin, you have set a standard that will be hard to replace."

It was very comforting to know I would be missed.

*(Note: Stefan Petersen is a pseudonym to protect the privacy of the individuals involved.)

Chapter 12

Married Life

You once said the man you married turned out to have serious emotional problems. Didn't you observe those during the courtship phase?

Unfortunately, I didn't. Stefan seemed very kind and caring during the six months before we married. Although I had been warned by my fiancé's boss that my future husband "gets a bit nervous," I just shrugged my shoulders. Once, too, my boss at SAS took me aside and said, "You should know that Stefan uses quite a bit of alcohol."

These warnings went unheeded; I was twenty-nine years old, two months pregnant, and in love. Stefan was charming and dynamic. I had been engaged twice before, so I thought I knew and understood men. Looking back, if I hadn't been pregnant, I would have probably waited to know him better before marrying him.

How long did your marriage last?

Four years. When I married Stefan, I felt very positive, but during the next four years, I became subdued and anxious, and, in the end, terrified. So, I left.

Weren't you married in the Catholic Church? Was it a big wedding?

We married in a Catholic church in Gothenburg, Sweden. Although I was still a Protestant, Stefan, born and raised in the Netherlands, was a practicing Catholic. We had a small, traditional wedding with less than a dozen friends in attendance.

When did you realize Stefan had major problems?

During the first few months of married life, Stefan and I didn't get along too well. I thought things would improve after I had our baby. As independent as I was, I became a docile wife to shield myself from Stefan's emotional outbursts. Also, I decided to convert to Catholicism because that was Stefan's religion. To meet the Catholic Church's requirements for conversion, I met with a priest once a week in Stockholm for six months after taking my marriage vows. Our daughter, Ingrid, was born in Stockholm. Stefan, by then, had been transferred to Amsterdam.

Did you tell any of your relatives about your marital difficulties?

I kept quiet about it. Although my mother was always very supportive of my decisions, I felt she didn't like Stefan. She seemed sad about this union. Despite her love and support, I knew she believed I had made one of life's major mistakes by picking the wrong man to marry.

You once told me that you really started praying to God because your marriage gave you such heartache?

Looking back on my married life, I remember it as a time in which I sought God fervently. Without question, I believe my marital difficulties helped me to find God. God promises us, "When you seek me with all your heart, I will let you find me."

It seems like a tough way to find God?

It was. During the first year of my marriage, I suffered terribly. Our Catholic priest kept advising me to remain calm and faithful to my husband which I tried to do. However, it became increasingly difficult to remain married.

Why? Was there a point when you knew you had to leave your husband?

When Stefan was transferred to a new job as a station manager at the airport in Madrid, my married life became unbelievably bad.

By then, Ingrid had turned four-years-old; and we lived in a nice house and had a maid. One night, the maid fried the meat too long, and it was tough. Stefan, Ingrid and I were eating dinner at home when suddenly Stefan picked the meat from his plate and threw it on the floor.

"It's too tough," he growled at me. I didn't dare say anything until Ingrid was in bed asleep.

"Stefan, please don't do things like that in front of our daughter," I pleaded.

Stefan picked up a glass of milk and threw it over me. Usually I was so scared, I never said or did anything to antagonize him. This time, however, I picked up my glass of half-finished milk and threw it over him.

With that, he walked into the kitchen, picked up the ax our maid used to chop firewood, and slammed it right through the radio on the kitchen counter, completely destroying it.

How horrifying. What did you say?

I was speechless.

"Now I'm going to leave," he yelled and started walking out the front door. But he changed his mind.

He changed his mind about leaving?

He then stepped back and walked into Ingrid's room, and announced, "I'm not going. You are going to have to leave."

I walked out, still covered with milk, and shaking with fear. A month before, he had pulled his Gurkha knives (two long knives used by famous soldiers who live near Nepal) off the wall and threw them at me. Fortunately, I ducked in time, and the knives hit the wall. I didn't want to risk another knife-throwing incident. Stefan displayed these knives (about five decimeters long with carved handles) on a wall in our house. The knives were souvenirs from his stint in the Dutch military when he had been stationed in Karachi, Pakistan during World War II.

He sounds very violent. What did you do?

I walked outside and took a bus to our priest's home. The priest called Stefan's doctor, who said he had dinner guests and could only see Stefan in the morning. Next, my priest called Stephan's boss, the commercial manager of a major airline. He, too, had guests; but he said I should come to his office the next morning. I said farewell to my priest and took a taxi to see my Swedish friend, Hilla Brita Thott, who was also living in Madrid. She gave me some cognac, and I slept in her spare bedroom. The next morning, I went to see Stefan's boss at his office.

You must have been so worried about your daughter? Did you call home?

The next morning, Hilla Brita called me at the office of Mr. Gouberville, Stefan's boss. She told me that Stefan had called her wanting to know where I had spent the night. Her call chilled my heart! Stefan told Hilla Brita that he had little Ingrid on his lap; he was drunk; and he had his Gurkha knives on the table in front of him. These knives are so sharp you can cut off the head of a cow with one strike.

What did Stefan's boss do? He must have been concerned, too?

He immediately left for our house with his driver and a medical doctor. About 45 minutes later, Stefan's boss appeared with Ingrid in his arms. She was just fine.

You must have felt so relieved?

It was the happiest moment of my life. The time had come, I decided, to leave my husband. I was tired of being frightened out of my wits.

You and Ingrid returned to Stockholm, and moved into an apartment on the outskirts of Stockholm in Nockeby, near Bromma. Were you getting any money from Stefan for living expenses?

No. I was giving English lessons to Swedes at my home.

Did Stefan try to make contact with you and Ingrid?

He did, but I didn't want to see him. Two years later, when Ingrid was six, our bishop called me and suggested I try to repair my marriage.

Stefan had visited him and convinced the Catholic bishop in Stockholm that it would be best if we were united as a family. Stefan was transferring to Istanbul, Turkey, and, if I would not come to Istanbul, then he wanted Ingrid to visit him in Turkey.

Were you reluctant to have Ingrid visit him in Turkey?

Yes. I agreed she could visit him in Holland at his mother's home for a couple of weeks in the summer. And, Ingrid spent a couple of weeks in Holland with her grandmother and saw her father. When she returned to Sweden, she told me that she had been praying that we should all be united as a family.

Didn't you make another effort at this marriage—for Ingrid's sake?

I had prayed long and hard about this separation and felt so despondent. Maybe, I thought, he had changed. So, I met Stefan in Stockholm, and we agreed to try married life again. I really wasn't sure he had changed though.

Stefan had taken a new job as an airline station manager in Amsterdam, and later we moved to Frankfurt, Germany. It was difficult situation because I was afraid of him.

Why were you afraid of him? Was he still drinking heavily? What did he do?

One evening, he threw a bottle at me. I went into our bedroom and moved my clothes into the guest bedroom. When he saw me do this, he went into Ingrid's room and opened the windows wide open.

"Don't do that," I pleaded. She might catch pneumonia."

He replied heatedly, "It might be just as well."

I closed Ingrid's bedroom window and retired to the guest bedroom. The next day, Stefan left for Amsterdam on business. I quickly packed and flew back to Stockholm, with Ingrid at my side. It had been a chilly December.

Didn't he come to Sweden looking for you?

Several days later, Stefan arrived in Stockholm with the priest from Frankfurt hoping to see me. I didn't see him as I was out looking for a job.

He telephoned me before leaving saying I could return to Germany to get the rest of my things. I left Ingrid with my sister and traveled to Germany to collect all my belongings.

Did you then get a divorce from him?

I obtained a separation through the Catholic Church, and, several years later, I agreed to a divorce so my ex-husband could remarry.

How did you feel about his new marriage? Were you totally liberated from this relationship and trying to find a new marriage partner for yourself?

Although I was divorced, I really didn't have any more romantic relationships after my divorce. I was getting older, and it was difficult to meet single men of a certain age. Also, I still had weekly nightmares about my difficult marriage. In fact, it was only many years later, when I was 48-years-old, that I finally achieved peace of mind after encountering a unique spiritual experience.

What kind of spiritual experience?

In 1968, I attended a special lecture at the Gustav Vasa Lutheran Church in Stockholm given by Demos Shakarian, an Armenian immigrant to America. Mr. Shakarian, a Christian, had fled to the United States from Armenia with his parents when he was six years old. They were fleeing the Turkish purges of the Armenian people following the collapse of the Ottoman Empire at the end of World War I. As a result of that extermination, many Armenians sought political refuge in the United States.

Mr. Shakarian had achieved the American dream: He was very rich! Initially, he built his financial empire as a farmer and owned one of the largest dairy farms in America. His fortune grew even larger when he started building shopping centers throughout the United States after World War II. Then, he had a spiritual revelation and founded the Full Gospel Businessman International organization in the mid-1960s. He and his colleagues traveled around the world preaching the gospel and conducting faith healing services in which some people were actually healed.

Did you see him actually heal someone in a church in Sweden?

No. It was his talk about forgiveness that brought about a spiritual healing inside of me. During the lecture I attended, Mr. Shakarian told his Stockholm audience about the importance of true forgiveness. He described how he had been in a tough business negotiation with a competitor.

He said he had been so tough hammering out a deal that he felt "victorious." Then, upon further reflection, he decided he had behaved in a very un-Christian manner. He telephoned his competitor, who was staying at a nearby hotel, and asked for another meeting.

When his competitor met him in the hotel lobby, Mr. Shakarian said, "I called you because I want to ask for your forgiveness." The man was so taken aback by this statement that tears came into his eyes.

For me, the story was moving. However, it wasn't the story, although moving, that changed my life; it was what happened to me during his lecture. As I sat in the church watching Mr. Shakarian speak, I noticed that everything in the church appeared as if it were made of gold. The angels and statues had actually turned gold in color.

You saw everything in the church turn gold in color?

The angels and statues in the church turned gold! When I looked at Mr. Shakarian's Swedish interpreter, everything appeared in its normal color. It was like watching color TV and then flipping the channel and seeing the same program on a black and white TV. This color change continued during the entire lecture. Immediately after hearing Mr. Shakarian's talk, I felt a keen desire to contact my former husband, and ask for forgiveness. I remembered sadly that Stefan lost his job and stopped going to church after we divorced.

How did you contact your former husband?

That evening I wrote to Stefan, asking him to forgive me

for causing him such hardship when I left. In a few days, I received a letter from him. He had addressed the envelope so quickly that my name and address were upside down.

The envelope contained a short note. It said, "Dear Karin, it took me a long time to forgive you and an even longer time to realize there was nothing to forgive. Jesus forgives more than anybody else. I wish you peace of mind and happiness."

Ever since I received that letter, I have had peace of mind. I believe my suffering brought me much closer to God. I realize now how much God loves us.

Looking back, is there any way your marriage could have been saved? Do you think you were doing something or saying something that made Stefan behave so badly?

I think I was too passive. If I had stood up to him and had not tried so hard to give in to his every mood, there may have been a chance to save our marriage. I don't know. He had emotional problems that were too difficult for me to withstand.

Chapter 13

Raising Ingrid

Since you did not receive any economic support from your husband, what jobs did you take to support yourself and Ingrid in Stockholm?

When I returned to Stockholm, after leaving my husband the first time, I taught English in my home in Bromma. I wanted to be at home with Ingrid, who was only four years old. During the holidays, I worked at Tipstjänst (the Swedish lottery) while a Swedish couple who lived on an island in the Stockholm Archipelago, looked after Ingrid. Ingrid loved being with them and their six children. I could work at Tipstjänst part-time, as well, if I needed extra money.

You worked at a rather menial job considering all the interesting jobs you once had. How did you feel?

My job was to look through all the lottery entries and try to find the winners. The work was monotonous, after the exciting positions I had held. Perhaps that was its purpose for me.

You once told me Stefan tried to send you money. Is that true?

During this time, I didn't want any money from him.

However, a friend told me that I should ask Stefan to provide money for Ingrid's education. So I did. He sent me money for her education until he remarried.

Which school did Ingrid attend?

When she turned five years old, Ingrid attended the French school in Stockholm. One of the nuns from the St. Joseph's Order was the director of the school then, so I felt quite secure.

What about your social life? Were you dating anyone during Ingrid's school-age years?

I was a single parent in the 1950s and 1960s when it was not nearly as common as it is today. Although my friends invited me to meet some of their men friends, I wasn't that interested in beginning any new relationships. I was really scared of becoming involved romantically because of my difficult marriage.

All-in-all, however, my social life wasn't too bad. I had many friends and received invitations to some very nice events. In 1956, I was invited to a tea to meet Her Royal Highness Queen Elizabeth II of England and her husband Prince Philip. This tea, which included about 100 people, was held at the Royal Tennis Club in Stockholm. I remember thinking the Queen looked far better in person than she did in photographs. She had lovely skin. Also, Prince Philip was very talkative and witty. There was always laughter and congeniality around the groups of people he spoke with at this event.

What was Ingrid like as a teenager? That is when most daughters and mothers have problems.

Ingrid, as a teenager, once told me her classmates were "fed up" with their mothers. But, she said, I was an "ok" mom. That made me feel really good! Ingrid often brought her friends to our house after school.

Did Ingrid attend the French school throughout her entire school career?

While we were in Germany, Ingrid started first grade at the Waldorf School, a private school system founded by the famous Austrian spiritual leader, Rudolf Steiner. The thrust of his program is to enhance a student's creativity. When we returned to Sweden, I placed her in the Kristopher School. This school was associated with the German Waldorf School. In the Steiner program, music and art play a key role; and Ingrid learned to play the flute and the guitar in school. When she was ready for high school, Ingrid chose The Nya Elementar Gymnasium (high school) in Bromma. There, she studied Russian and decided to pursue a Foreign Service career.

What university did Ingrid attend?

During the early 1970s, Ingrid attended the University of Stockholm and took degrees in Pedagogy, Russian and English. Deciding she needed a break from academia, Ingrid took off for six months to train as a riding instructor in England. It was and still is very common for Swedish students to take a six-month break from their studies at a university to work in a particular field or travel. When Ingrid graduated from the University of Stockholm in 1973, she quickly got a job with the United Nations Educational, Scientific, and Cultural Organization's (UNESCO) International Bureau of Education in Geneva. She had such a good salary that she paid off her university loans in two years.

What were you doing when Ingrid was older? You once told me you wanted to take a job helping people? Did you do this?

I decided I wanted to do more to help people, so I accepted a position with a small volunteer organization, Svalorna, which helped the poor in Latin America. My job was to screen student applicants who wanted to spend a year in that program.

Did you have friends working at Svalorna?

Suzanne Sandberg, my best friend, started Svalorna. I had known Suzanne since my days at SAS when she had married a pilot I knew. Suzanne's sister had married a wealthy Swede who lived in Peru. Once, when Suzanne was visiting her sister in South America, she saw many women in Lima, rummaging through garbage, trying to find something to eat. She decided to start an organization to help poor women. When she returned to Sweden, she founded Svalorna, an organization that financially supported young Swedes who wanted to work in Latin America for one year as day care workers. By taking jobs watching over these children, Swedish students were a big help to women who wanted to get trained for jobs. This was an idealistic and caring organization, but it had very little money.

Didn't you return to your old organization, the Swedish Red Cross?

Because I needed more money, I had to leave Svalorna. For the first few months in 1962, I worked as the secretary to the medical advisor of the Swedish Red Cross. When my boss's secretary returned from leave, I switched to the international section of the organization.

Following that two-year period, you accepted a job as the Head of the Refugee Department for Arbetsförmeldlingen (Swedish Governmental Employment Agency) and held this job for six years and had four people working for you. How would you describe this undertaking?

Very tough. I needed a much larger staff because it was during this period that Sweden received thousands of immigrants from countries around the world.

What groups were immigrating to Sweden during this period?

In 1970, the Swedish government allowed 2,350 Polish Jews to immigrate to Sweden because they were being oppressed by the Communists in Poland. Also, there were Americans requesting political asylum because they wanted to avoid the draft and fighting in the Vietnam War. In addition, we had refugees fleeing to Sweden from the Communist regimes in Hungary, Poland and Czechoslovakia.

Then, in 1973, there was a coup in Chile; and Sweden agreed to accept 6,000 Chilean immigrants fleeing political persecution in that country. By the end of 1973, there were 24 refugee camps for Chileans all over Sweden. And, they all needed jobs as soon as they learned Swedish. I was working 14-hour days for months at a time

Didn't you request more help?

I kept pressing my boss for more staff but never received any extra help. As it happened, some of my staff had health problems, and couldn't work overtime. I finally left the job as head of the refugee department because of the long working hours and took a less demanding position in the information department of Arbetsförmedlingen.

Interestingly enough, after you left, the Refugee Department hired a lot more people.

I suppose the lesson I learned there was this: Hard work for good causes often must be considered as its own reward.

Did you retire from this job?

In 1985, I retired and became a pensioner. Although I retired from a paying job, I didn't retire from life. I'm still actively visiting sick and suffering people, volunteering at Caritas (Swedish Catholic Charity) visiting the Stockholm jail once a week, and until last year, I worked at the soup kitchen in Stockholm. My doctor advised me to cut down on some activities, so I decided to rest on Friday, the day I usually helped in the soup kitchen.

What do you consider to be your greatest accomplishment?

Looking at my life, I consider my greatest accomplishment

to be my daughter. Ingrid was a very easy child to raise, and we've always been close friends.

Did you ever have any major disagreements with your child?

I think our only disagreement pertained to the neatness of her room; I always thought it was too messy.

But a messy room it not a major problem. I never had to remind Ingrid to do her homework. She was a very responsible and bright child. In fact, one of the strictest teachers at her school in Bromma told me, "It must be wonderful to be the mother of Ingrid."

"Yes," I said, "It is!"

What does Ingrid do now?

She is a psychologist in Holland.

Chapter 14

Finding a Purpose

What is your basic philosophy of life?

My basic philosophy is, "do unto others as you would have them do unto you." For many years, I was a member of the Swedish state church, and although I knew about Christ, I didn't think religion made much difference in my life. When my teenage friends were confirmed and received Holy Communion, I did not join them. I belonged to the Lutheran Church, but I never took part in any activities.

So you never read any religious books until you became Catholic?

When I converted to Catholicism, I began reading about the saints in the church. The ones who have inspired me the most are St. Teresa of Avila, St. Teresa of the Child Jesus (also known as St. Teresa of Lisieux), and, especially, St. Francis of Assisi.

Why these particular saints?

I love St. Teresa's message, "He who possesses God, lacks nothing; God alone suffices in your life." She also wrote, "Inner prayer seems to be nothing but a friendly intercourse and diligent conversation in solitude with the One whom we know loves us."

Also, I greatly admire St. Teresa of the Child Jesus, popularly known as "the Little Flower."

She was born in Normandy, France in 1873 and died at the young age of 24. She epitomized Mathew 18:2: "Unless you change your lives and become like little children, you will not enter the kingdom of Heaven."

St. Francis of Assisi, who died in 1225, is unique among the saints not only because he received the stigmata, but especially because of his likeness to Christ in his lifestyle and apostolate. I recall reading that St. Francis once met a leper who was covered with sores. At first he was appalled. But God touched his heart and changed his disgust into love. He embraced this leper, and the leper was instantly cured.

In your work for Mother Teresa, have you ever met someone who totally disgusted you?

I've never met anyone who totally disgusted me, but I've met people who have tried my patience. About seven years ago, I visited a woman who had been identified in a weekly Swedish tabloid magazine as "the loneliest person in Sweden." I had received a call from the editor of the magazine who gave me her name and asked me to visit her.

I called her, and we picked a day to meet. I took the subway to her neighborhood outside of Stockholm and found her flat. When she came to the door, she was wearing a tattered sweater and was half-dressed (in her slip). Her hair was dirty and tangled. Although it was a sunny day, all the blinds on her apartment windows were down, and she had locked the door to her sitting room which meant we could only sit in the small kitchen of her two-room flat.

What did you talk about?

I didn't talk, she did! She talked fervently, as though she had been starved for someone to listen to her. She told me she "hated everything and everybody." She "hated" the social workers who came to visit her. She "hated" the neighborhood. She "hated" her flat. Although she had difficulty in walking and was in her 80's, she seemed in fairly good health. I didn't say much. On my second visit with her, I again listened to her complain about her neighbors, her flat, and her life.

At the end of my second visit, which was about 90 minutes, I asked her, "Do you know the Lord's Prayer?" She said, "Yes." I said, "Let's pray it together." She nodded. So, we did. And, I wished her peace, and told her I would see her in a week.

I suppose you were not looking forward to the next visit with this lady?

Not really. But, an interesting thing happened. The next time I went to see her; she had totally changed. She had someone visit and fix her hair. She was wearing a nice, clean dress. Her window blinds were up and her flat was clean. She invited me to her sitting room which previously had been locked up.

The first thing she asked, as I sat down was, "Would it be difficult to give my clothes to Mother Teresa's Order in India?"

"It's not at all difficult, "I replied, adding that I would be happy to collect her donation during my next visit.

And, during that visit, she gave me several big bags filled with nice, used clothes. She only lived four months after that meeting, but I felt so happy knowing she had found God before she died.

Why aren't more Swedes volunteering like you and trying to make a difference?

They are starting to realize that life is very empty unless you help others. I'm starting to see more people volunteering. And, it's so needed! I've discovered that most sick and suffering people really need someone who will listen. They need to discuss their problems. When I receive a call from someone who is sick and needs a visitor, I go to that person, and we chat. I usually listen more than anything else.

I sense that people would like to do something, but they don't know how. Several people have asked to accompany me when I visit the Sick and Suffering, but it's difficult. The Sick and Suffering are very sensitive and many feel insecure in front of strangers.

Haven't you had some Sick and Suffering people who are not native Swedes and enjoy speaking English?

Yes. When I have had Sick and Suffering Co-Workers who want to speak English, I can easily find a volunteer to come with me for the visit.

Why aren't there more Co-Workers like you in Sweden? You have so many people to visit and call?

That's just the way it was set up. The Order believes only one person should be responsible for the Sick and Suffering. There is usually one link for every country. That is the way it was originally organized.

But, aren't you in charge of Sick and Suffering in 4 countries in Scandinavia?

Yes. I am, for the moment.

Have you ever met someone who was simply impossible to talk with?

It's interesting that since 1976, I've met only two people who couldn't get over their bitterness in life. Most of the people I visit usually become members of Mother Teresa's Sick and Suffering network. They are united with one of Mother Teresa's sisters or brothers (throughout the world) for whom they pray.

How do you find lonely and sick people to visit?

People call me because they have read about me in a Catholic magazine. Or one of the Catholic priests calls and gives me the name of someone who needs a visitor. Since January 2000, I have two new people to visit following a phone conversation with Father Hererra, who is from Mexico, and a minister at St. Eugenia's Catholic Church in Stockholm. I contacted him after I received a letter from one of Mother Teresa's Brothers who was seeking a Spanish speaker who was a member of the sick and suffering network. He wanted that person to pray for him in Sweden. My two new people, who live in Stockholm, speak both Spanish and Swedish.

You have given talks about Mother Teresa and the meaning of life and finding God. How do you pray?

Each morning when I awake, I pray: "Here I am Lord, do with me as you wish." I cannot have peace or tranquility if I become upset by problems, so I don't. I just put everything in God's hands. I believe it really helps to talk to God personally, as if he were your best friend. Also, I know that once you find true peace, it is not easily lost.

Have you met anyone in Sweden who has had a very positive impact on your life spiritually?

Yes. Her name is Vassula Ryden, and she is a Greek Orthodox mystic and author of the book, *True Life in God.* I first heard about this book from Bob Carroll, the leader of a prayer group I joined in Stockholm eight years ago. Bob Carroll, now deceased, worked for a time at the American Embassy in Stockholm.

Vassula's message moved me deeply. She says Jesus is guiding her hand in putting his words on paper.

It's interesting that Vassula is Greek Orthodox, and she rarely attended church before 1986. However, since 1986, she has written 17 books which have been described by numerous priests — Catholic, Orthodox, and Protestant—as "a valuable record of mystical experience." Do you believe she is absolutely valid and not "making this up?"

I'm absolutely sure. Vassula said she asked Jesus why he had chosen her to write his words as she knew nothing of church matters. Jesus said to her, "Because you are a 'nothing,' I can be everything."

Jesus appeared one day to Vassula when she was living in Bangladesh with her husband and children. Her husband, who is Swedish, works for an international aid organization, and Vassula was a socialite housewife living a somewhat pampered life. When she started receiving Jesus' words, she was startled.

I guess she was startled. What did she do when she started getting messages from Jesus?

She wrote down all of his words. One of the visions Jesus gave her was three solid metal bars. Then Jesus led her to understand that the three bars represented the three Christian churches— Protestant, Catholic, and Orthodox. He asked her, "How can these bars meet?" He also answered the question,"They should bend to be able to unite. To bend, iron must be softened."

Jesus told her the Holy Spirit's fire would unite everyone. But before that happens, Vassula said, Jesus would like all Christians to work toward unity and to agree to have one date for Easter. The Eastern Orthodox Church, which has about 250 million followers worldwide, celebrates its holiest day on its own calendar. The Orthodox Church follows the Jewish calendar, on the reasoning that the Last Supper was a Seder and that the Resurrection should, therefore, follow Passover. Every few years, the two Easters coincide, but usually they are a few weeks apart.

Are her books selling worldwide?

Vassula's books are published in 32 languages, and she has visited thousands of people around the world. Her mission is to restore Christian unity, and I believe her ministry will continue to grow.

Do many people in Sweden know about her?

More and more people are becoming aware of her and reading her books. I read that Swedish Prime Minister Goran Persson said if he had not become a politician, he would have become a priest. I felt he should know about Vassula, so I recently sent him a letter and her book, *True Life in God.*

Has the Prime Minister read the book?

I received a letter from his office. He has not had time to read the book, but he was very appreciative of my efforts to send it.

Let's discuss the clergy in Sweden. Are they doing anything to raise issues of injustice and unethical behavior?

They are doing much too little. They should be doing a lot more!

Who are the Swedes and where do they want to be? They are very secular and don't seem to be interested in religion. Is that changing?

I think Swedes put science and technology at the top of their list. That really bothers me, and it is not only happening in Sweden. I believe too many people live in this world without knowing what to live for. Living without a reason is not living, it is existing. In the end you have to listen to your heart. As Vassula Ryden, who gets regular messages from Jesus, suggests, "We should do everything in union with Him all through the day."

How has God helped you?

He has helped me in many ways, but let me give you one, simple example. For several years I have been asked to speak publicly about my work with Mother Teresa's organization. I used to fear public speaking and became very nervous before each speech. Now, I'm calm at any public speaking event because I've asked God to be with me. In my prayers right before I give a talk, I ask God, "please, speak through me." Now, it is very easy to speak to any group.

You are a very active volunteer. Why did you begin volunteering in the Stockholm prison?

Besides visiting the sick and suffering, one of the most gratifying things I do every week is visit the Stockholm jail. I started visiting prisoners in the Stockholm jail as the official representative of the Swedish Red Cross 12 years ago. I had a friend who visited prisoners there, and I asked her how I could participate. She said I had to be officially screened by the prison authorities before I would be allowed to visit a prisoner.

To comply with Swedish government regulations, one has to be politically and religiously neutral. That means the only way I can mention anything about God or the Christian faith is if the prisoner initiates such a conversation. Also, I do not wear a cross when I visit the prison as I must conform to the prison's visitation policy.

Do you think Swedes are educated to be good? To think about other people?

Yes. But today the rules are not as strongly enforced. There have been major changes in society during the last 20 years.

Is it the influence of TV? The lack of church attendance? Why has society changed?

TV has had a negative impact because of the violence. Also, the Swedish government has banned the Ten Commandments from the schools.

Why?

The government is following the modern trend throughout the Western world to accommodate every religious belief, so they can't promote the Christian Bible. Children don't learn about Christianity the way it was taught when I was attending school in the 1930s. In Sweden, Christianity is seen in Sweden as nothing better or worse than all the other religions.

Is that affecting society?

Unfortunately, today's society reflects the decline of Christian teachings. After I visited a young man in prison who had murdered a young boy in a quite gruesome manner, I saw former Swedish Prime Minister Ingvar Carlsson that night on television saying "We, the Social Democrats, want law and order," and so forth.

Didn't you write Prime Minister Carlsson a letter about the growing crime problem in Sweden?

Yes, I did. In the letter, I wrote, "The Social Democratic Party has been reigning in Sweden for 40 years, and it has taken away a meaningful Christian education in the schools. The students don't learn the Ten Commandments, so now they kill and shoplift and have many sexual partners."

Shortly thereafter, Mr. Carlsson sent me a two-page typed letter in which he wrote: "One can't put the whole social responsibility on the schools and the government."

Did you write a follow-up letter to him?

No, because he thought the students should learn from their parents at home, but the problem remains: Swedish parents haven't had any Christian education either. It's been like this for 40 years!

What do you think about the world coming to an end in our lifetime? Are we living in the end times?

Many have said we are in the final days of earth's existence. People talk about three dark days, and then everything comes to an end. Even scholars in biblical prophecy seem to focus on the "Great Tribulation" rather than on the positive features of the Kingdom of God where the lion lays down with the lamb. People are very pessimistic about the future today.

It's curious that in a time of incredible material benefits, with restraints on personal behavior practically non-existent, that people are not happy or confident about the future. Why?

In order to break out of the mold that our problems are beyond us, we need to turn to God. We need God's grace, but it is not something we can manipulate or generate on our own; it must come from God.

What do you think about the future? Are you pessimistic?

When you know that you are loved by Our Father, you can't have any real worries. "Do not worry," says Jesus, "Your father knows what you need." (Matthew 6: 31-32) A true conversion consists of turning away from the surface and turning toward the depths of yourself, where God dwells.

I don't think about the future. I leave everything in God's hands. I try to live in the present. By living in the here and now, I don't worry. Each day, I read a passage from Brother Wilfrid's Stinissen's book, *Idag är Gud's Dag* (Today is God's Day). I try to live by his words: "It is very important to live fully in the present, to make the very best of just this moment. Do not worry about the future, nor fret over the past."

So, as it is written in the Bible, "Rejoice always, pray continuously, and thank God for everything." I try to live that way, and I am happy and at peace.